PAT JENNINGS

PAT JENNINGS

AN AUTOBIOGRAPHY

PAT JENNINGS
IN ASSOCIATION WITH REG DRURY

WILLOW BOOKS
Collins
8 Grafton Street, London W1
1983

Willow Books
William Collins Sons & Co Ltd
London · Glasgow · Sydney · Auckland
Toronto · Johannesburg

First published 1983
© Pat Jennings 1983

British Library Cataloguing in Publication Data

Drury, Reg
Pat Jennings
1. Jennings, Pat   2. Soccer players –
Northern Ireland – Biography
I. Title
796.334'092'4   GV942.7.J/

ISBN 0–00–218069–3

Filmset in Plantin
by Ace Filmsetting Ltd, Frome, Somerset
Printed and bound in Great Britain by
Wm Collins Sons & Co Ltd, Glasgow

CONTENTS

1 CROSSING THE WATER 1

2 MOVING TO SPURS 12

3 GENTLEMAN JIM and other Spurs characters 22

4 'WE'VE DECIDED TO LET YOU GO' 36

5 JOINING THE 'LONDON IRISH' 46

6 THE IDEAL PARTNERSHIP 56

7 HOOLIGANISM 66

8 BOUQUETS AND BRICKBATS 77

9 ON GOALKEEPERS AND GOALKEEPING 89

10 WEMBLEY 101

11 FUN AND GAMES ABROAD 111

12 GEORGE BEST 120

13 UNITED IRELAND 129

14 WORLD CUP EUPHORIA 140

15 SO NEAR AND YET SO FAR 150

16 LOOKING AHEAD 160

CAREER AT A GLANCE 170

1

CROSSING THE WATER

There is a sports complex in my home town of Newry, County Down, which includes a couple of soccer pitches. It is called 'Jennings Park' and I am very proud that when it was built the local council decided to name it after me. Nothing I may have achieved in football has given me more pleasure. Although I'm a Londoner by adoption, I always enjoy going back to Newry where my parents, most of my family and many of my friends still live.

It was on the site of Pat Jennings Park, when it was a meadow without even dressing rooms, that I played my first competitive games. I still remember vividly the tears I shed when my team reached a cup final and I was dropped because I was too small and too young.

In fact, I was only 11 and playing in a league for boys under 19, so I was by far the youngest among the 12 or so teams taking part. But I was the regular goalkeeper for Shamrock Rovers (all the sides were named after famous clubs) and I had only one handicap – my size. I didn't let in many low shots; yet since I couldn't even touch the crossbar when I jumped as high as I could, I have to admit I was frequently beaten by the simplest of lobs. It made life difficult on days when a fierce wind was blowing straight down the pitch.

We took our football seriously and couldn't have put more effort into each game if it had been an FA Cup final at Wembley, instead of on the old meadow where goal posts were a luxury and you rubbed yourself down with a towel after the match and then ran home with most of the mud still clinging.

Soccer was banned at my school, but the local league was always the big topic of conversation. And because I was playing with older lads, I used to get the star treatment from my classmates. If I had had a particularly good game the previous evening, they would embarrass me by cheering and clapping when I turned up at school in the morning. That landed me in more than one spot of bother with the teachers when I was a bit late and trying to creep in unnoticed.

Sometimes more than 1000 people turned up to see a game, a tremendous crowd in the relatively small town of Newry, so you can imagine the extent of the local interest. It also gives you some idea of how I felt when the two men who ran Rovers, Ritchie Hollywood and Frank O'Hanlon, came to their reluctant decision to leave me out of the team for the final after I had played in all the previous rounds. I suppose I understood their reasoning that the team would have more chance with a bigger boy in goal, but it seemed so unfair. Even though I was eventually presented with a medal, I felt let down. I didn't dream, then, that there were Wembley finals in store. I just thought I'd missed the biggest game of my life.

There was no second chance the following season, for the league was disbanded and it was to be five years before I again took part in organized soccer. I turned to Gaelic football with my school, but each morning the Jennings family still had a regular kick-about in the yard attached to our house.

My sister Marie, the only girl among seven boys, was frequently pressganged into playing to make up the numbers and she took her share of knocks on the concrete surface. Now Marie works for Aer Lingus and can afford to smile when people say that she must have been really spoiled as an only daughter with so many brothers to protect her. Marie had an extra chore, sewing patches on the football my father used to buy us for Christmas when it became worn on the rough ground. It rarely lasted beyond January and then we had to make do with a tennis ball for our morning 'matches'.

My eldest brother Brian was responsible for my soccer comeback at the age of 16. Brian was a winger who went on to become a regular amateur international with Northern Ireland, and could easily have made the grade as a professional in England. But he complied with my parents' wishes to concentrate upon his education, got his degree at Manchester University and is now a schoolteacher. So he remained an amateur throughout a lengthy Irish League career with Coleraine and only hung up his boots a year or two ago.

At the time Brian was playing for Newry United, the reserve team of our Irish 'B' League club Newry Town. Mid-way through season 1961–62 they had a goalkeeper problem because the first choice was leaving, so Brian talked me into attending a training session. I was offered a game the following Saturday.

When I turned out on a freezing cold afternoon, with the pitch covered in two inches of snow, I began to have my doubts for I was sure I could have found a better way of spending my time. But we won 1–0 and I was hooked. The team went from strength to strength and, against all the odds, won the Irish Junior Cup. Now I had a medal I had really earned.

2

The start of the following season saw me promoted to the Newry Town side, and I must have shaped up reasonably well because after a few months the chairman took me to one side and said he had recommended me for the trials for the Northern Ireland youth team which was due to go to England in April to play in the European youth championships – the little World Cup. I told him I was grateful, and certainly flattered, but I wasn't interested. England seemed a long way to me. I had never travelled out of Ireland and didn't relish the thought of leaving home.

That might have been the end of the matter had not Newry been drawn against Crusaders, big shots from Belfast, in the Irish Cup. I had a particularly good game, despite a 2–1 defeat, and afterwards the Crusaders' chairman – who was in charge of the national youth team selection committee – came to see me and said he'd be delighted to have me in the Northern Ireland side.

The trip to England wasn't a formality. First we had to qualify against the Republic of Ireland in home and away matches, and only managed it by the odd goal with a 3–2 victory after a 1–1 draw. Now we were all set for the Hi-de-hi treatment, for the 16 teams taking part in the little World Cup were housed at Butlin's Holiday Camp at Bognor Regis.

When I left Belfast, one of a happy bunch of 16 Irish youngsters, I had no thought that by the end of the month I would be launched on a professional career. So far as I was concerned I was setting out on a footballing holiday.

I was content enough with my life at the time, working with my father for a timber firm in Newry and earning under a fiver a week. I had failed my 11-plus exam, left school at 15 and worked as a bobbin boy at a spinning mill for ten months before being made redundant. That was when my father got me the job in the timber yard, one of the biggest in Ireland.

I enjoyed the open air life. Swinging a hatchet or using a saw to trim the branches off a tree on a summer's day seemed to be a good way of earning a living and I didn't have a care in the world. Even the cold weather didn't really bother me, though I'm bound to admit that helping to load timber on to a lorry at Belfast Docks in mid-winter did leave your fingers numb. And sitting on top of a pile of logs on an open lorry for the trip back to Newry left other parts of your anatomy frozen as well.

The job could be a bit dangerous at times. More than once a tree weighing three tons or more would slip its chains when it was being

3

hauled up on a crane and come crashing down. Looking back, I can only think my positional sense kept me out of trouble. Wielding a hatchet could be tricky, too, if the tree on which you were standing suddenly spun round. It happened to me once, I missed the log and hit my boot instead. The blade of the axe went right between my toes but didn't even break the skin. That was sheer good fortune, and I guess I was also lucky to avoid a serious mishap with a saw. Most of the sawyers I know have the top of a finger missing.

So I missed the pitfalls and benefited from the advantages of a job which was ideal for body building as well as sharpening the reflexes. I wasn't fired by any ambition to do anything else, and it hadn't occurred to me I was good enough to make a living playing football. Until I arrived at Butlin's.

Four of the Northern Ireland players in our youth squad were already on the books of English clubs. Dave Clements – who later became first a player and then manager of the full Irish team – was with Wolves; John Napier at Bolton; Tommy McKeowen and Sammy Todd both with Burnley. Ten of the remaining 12 had been signed by Irish League clubs, which left the two goalkeepers as the only players not with a senior side. My understudy Tommy Stokes played for Post Office Sports.

Training went so well that I began to wonder if I might get an opportunity to catch the attention of a scout from an English club. But I didn't let it keep me awake at nights. To reach the semi-final stage of the tournament we had to finish on top of a group which included Belgium, Czechoslovakia and Sweden. Everybody rated the Irish as outsiders, including the Irish players. Not that it mattered. Enjoying the experience was the name of the game. Our manager Norman Kernaghan and trainer Freddie Jardine, both smashing fellows, asked no more of us than we all did our best.

Perhaps our relaxed approach, while most of the other teams – and especially those from behind the Iron Curtain – were put under constant pressure to uphold the prestige of their country, gave us an advantage in a typically Irish way; maybe we genuinely under-estimated the all-round ability of our own side. Whatever the reason, we got off to a flying start by beating Belgium 2–1 at Eastbourne and followed up with a 1–0 win over the Czechs at Woking. A point from the remaining group game with Sweden at Bromley was all we needed for a semi-final spot and we duly drew 3–3. Northern Ireland had exceeded all expectations and, instead of returning home as provision-ally planned, it was on to Southampton to meet Bulgaria.

Most First Division footballers will tell you that The Dell isn't renowned for being one of the most palatial grounds in the League. It is such a tight enclosure that the crowd seems to be breathing down your neck and the actual playing pitch appears to be smaller than it is because the fans are so close. But when we arrived there on that April day in 1963 it seemed a fabulous place. It was like Wembley to us.

It looked like being the nearest we would get to Wembley when the Bulgarians scored the first goal of the game just four minutes from the end, but the luck of the Irish held. We equalized with a couple of minutes to go and when the score was still 1–1 after extra time, we won on the toss of a coin.

The Youth final was a night to remember. Under the Wembley floodlights, Northern Ireland went down 4–0 to a strong England side which was captained by Chelsea's Ronnie Harris and included players of the calibre of Liverpool's Tommy Smith, Arsenal's Jon Sammels and West Ham's John Sissons.

England did get one important break when our centre-half John Napier headed into his own goal to give them the lead. It was such a disappointment that our right-half Jimmy Nicholl from Coleraine, a wholehearted player who was always willing to run himself into the ground and didn't take kindly to losing, almost came to blows with poor John in the heat of the moment. As well as that, two of the Irish regulars were carrying injuries and shouldn't have played, but how could you deny a lad his big chance after he has battled right through the earlier rounds? Manager Kernaghan didn't have the heart to do it, and he had the support of the entire team. Anyway, I do not think for a moment that our walking wounded affected the final result as England were so much stronger. They deserved their victory, and Northern Ireland acquitted themselves with honour.

So the great adventure was over. We went back home and I returned to the more mundane task of lopping trees – but only for a single day. When I turned up at Newry's ground for training that night it was to be greeted by our chairman with the words: 'How do you fancy going to England full-time?' He told me that Watford had agreed a fee and that I would be getting £15 a week – unbelievable money since it was treble my pay at the timber yard.

I wasn't totally surprised. Northern Ireland's progress in the little World Cup had received wide newspaper coverage, and I had read that I had been watched on several occasions by Watford scout Bill McCracken. I knew the name because Bill, then nearing his 80th birthday, was something of a soccer folk hero in Belfast. He had been a full-back with Ireland and Newcastle in the early days of the century and was so smart at operating an offside trap that he caused the laws of the game to be revised in order to increase the scoring rate.

Originally a forward was offside unless there were three opponents, including the goalkeeper, between him and the goal when the ball was last played. So many clubs copied McCracken's successful tactics that the rule was changed to two opponents, and that still applies today although it seems the problem remains.

Bill naturally took a special interest in the Irish players during the youth tournament in England, and had been sufficiently impressed to recommend me to his chief scout, Stan Berry. It was Stan who was flying to Ireland to sign me.

My first reaction was to say 'No!' I didn't know which division Watford played in, and, anyway, I'd heard a hint that Coventry City – managed by Jimmy Hill – were also keen. I was prepared to wait. But although Jimmy has since told me he was ready to negotiate for my transfer, despite having his enthusiasm dampened slightly by a report that I was a bit on the small side for a lad of 17, he wasn't encouraged by Newry. They had come to an agreement with Watford and wanted to complete the deal as soon as possible.

I hesitated, partly because I still didn't fancy leaving my home and my family, but when Stan Berry turned up he painted such a convincing picture of Watford and what the future held for me that I agreed. Collecting a couple of quid expenses from Newry after a game had always seemed like a small fortune. But £15? That was almost the same as winning the pools.

Today a First Division player wouldn't think twice about paying £15 for a couple of rounds of drinks, but it represented big money when I was a teenager. Supplemented by bonus payments for a win or a draw, it allowed me to send cash home each week to my mother – who needed every penny she got to bring up a large family.

My father was never out of work when we were growing up, so we didn't go hungry. But we weren't exactly well off, either. That's why, when I was at school, I did all sorts of jobs on Saturdays and Sundays to earn the odd pound. I chopped up logs and sold bundles of firewood, at one old penny a time, and thought nothing of spending 12 hours a day picking blackberries or rose-hips to sell to local shops. I helped on a milk round and was a delivery boy for a grocer in the town.

Somehow, I don't think I was cut out to be a milkman. My employer, Peter Woods, knew I wasn't the day I jumped off the milk cart to deliver a couple of pints and caught my trouser bottoms on the top of a crate. I can still see the anguish on Peter's face as he surveyed three crates of broken milk bottles spread all over the road. He didn't ask if I was hurt, he just called me all the names that sprang to his mind – there were quite a few, some of which I hadn't even heard before.

I didn't have any mishaps on my grocery round, just aches and pains. All the stuff was loaded on a carrier at the front of an old-fashioned bike, and it was so heavy that instead of riding everywhere I had to spend half my time pushing that bike up the many hills in and around Newry.

Even when I left school and went to work, I always handed my pay packet to my mother on a Friday. She would give me five or ten shillings to spend – and I never felt I needed any more. That feeling of being able to pull my weight in the family was enough in those days. I wouldn't expect today's lad of 16 to understand; it's simply the way it was at that time. I'm sure I was no different to hundreds of thousands of boys of my age all over Britain. I was merely lucky that soccer opened up a new way of life.

Although I was suddenly 'rich' when I arrived at Watford, I was so overcome by homesickness that many a night I swore I would pack up and return to Ireland. Two things prevented me ending my career almost before it had begun. The first was my love of football: I enjoyed the atmosphere of being with a League club. The second was that I stayed with Stan Berry and his wife, who both did so much to try and make me feel at home. Stan liked his pint and he used to take me out in the evenings to prevent me feeling bored. I'd drink an orange or a coke and listen to his tales of soccer old-timers and some of the stunts he had used to sign promising players.

It was near the end of the season when I went to Watford and the club was struggling to avoid relegation to the Fourth Division. Once they were safe, I replaced Dave Underwood in goal for the two final matches.

I actually made my Football League debut for Watford on a ground where few other players have kicked a ball. It was against Queen's Park Rangers at the famous White City stadium and the result was a 2–2 draw.

That was in April 1963 when Rangers were experimenting by staging home matches at White City as a possible alternative to their own ground a couple of hundred yards away. In those days White City could hold more than 50,000, but it was too vast for Third

7

Division football with only several thousand fans dotted around the place. It lacked atmosphere and I wasn't surprised when Rangers went back to Loftus Road, then a run-down ground with a small wooden stand. It proved a wise long-term decision, for Loftus Road has since been transformed into one of the most compact grounds in the country with stands on all four sides – and seats for two-thirds of the spectators.

White City had been the venue when Britain's Derek Ibbotson had established a new world-record time for the mile. It was later used for a World Cup game between France and Uruguay in 1966, but now is mainly confined in sporting terms to greyhound meetings and houses the annual Greyhound Derby.

While I can hardly think of White City in the same way as Derek Ibbotson, and countless other famous athletes who had their moments of glory there, it has a special place in my footballing life as the ground where I conceded my very first League goal.

Ronnie Burgess was Watford's manager, a real gentleman who, to tell the truth, was too gentle for a job which needs a thick skin and a tough approach. Ronnie had been a great player with Spurs, as left-half and captain of the push-and-run side which won the Second and First Division championships in successive seasons, as well as being an automatic choice for Wales. Even then, at the age of 46, he was a bit useful when he played five-a-side games in the car park at Vicarage Road.

But things changed that summer. When I returned for pre-season training I left my temporary home with the Berrys and moved into new digs, where I was equally well looked after by a Mrs Dollard. And I found that Watford had a new manager – a real hard man called Bill McGarry.

The contrast with Ronnie Burgess couldn't have been more extreme. Bill, a former England wing-half, was a whirlwind. If he wasn't too pleased with the way the team performed he would kick the door open like a gunfighter from a Western film. He could also turn the air blue, and a few players' faces bright red, with his scathing comments.

Bill came from Bournemouth, where he had been player-manager. Watford was his first non-playing job – later he was to graduate to Ipswich, Wolves and Newcastle – and he was determined to make a success of it. His impact was immediate and in that 1963–64 season we finished third in the Third Division, missing promotion by a single place because only two clubs went up at that time.

Watford undoubtedly adopted a tougher outlook under McGarry.

Even the five-a-side games were often bruising affairs, with Bill joining in and neither asking nor granting any favours. He would moan at players who he felt had given less than a hundred per cent on a Saturday, but never complained at the treatment he got in training. Once, after a crunching tackle from Brian Owen, the boss had to be carried off and we all feared he had broken a leg. But next morning he was limping around and shouting his head off as usual.

I liked Bill. He was my kind of man, dead straight in all his dealings. He used to tell people that he didn't know if I had an Irish accent because I never opened my mouth in a match. But he couldn't have been more sympathetic in helping me settle into League football and gave me tremendous encouragement.

That season Watford played 51 League and Cup games and I didn't miss a single game. It was only after the last match – which, as it turned out, was to be my last for the club – that Bill was really critical of my performance.

It was at Luton, which counts as a local 'derby' for Watford, and we needed to win by two or three goals to have an outside chance of promotion. We lost 2–1 and I thought I did reasonably well, but Bill faulted me for one of the goals. 'You will never be a goalkeeper, son, until you've had your head kicked in a couple of times,' he announced in the dressing room. It was a characteristic McGarry statement, but it's one bit of advice I have managed to ignore in later years. I happen to think that the good goalkeepers are those who don't get their head kicked in.

It was while I was with Watford that I got my first full cap for Northern Ireland, but I got another honour that season when the triumphant England youth team which had won the little World Cup staged a celebration match at Wembley against the Rest of Britain. I was picked for the combined Irish, Scots and Welsh side, and it came as a pleasant surprise to be preferred to Gary Sprake who was then a first-team regular with Leeds.

Unfortunately, it wasn't a very happy return to Wembley on a wet and windy night. I had a miserable first half and we were 4–0 down at the interval before starting a revival of sorts and eventually losing 5–2.

I had changed my mud-covered jersey at half-time and at the end of the match one of the white-coated dressing-room attendants, who brought in the mugs of hot tea, came over to pat me on the back and deliver the most back-handed compliment of all time. 'Well done, you were terrific,' he said, 'much better than the other goalkeeper in the first half. He was terrible.'

My wife Eleanor likes to remind me of that story. To her it sums up the fluctuating fortunes of football – up one minute and down the next. Eleanor understands better than most because she was a singer and soccer can be a lot like show business.

Eleanor is a Newry girl but, although we knew each other by sight, we didn't really meet until I was a Tottenham player. I was home for the close-season break and went to a dance at the town hall where she was singing for the Hilton Show Band. We were introduced afterwards at the nearby fish-and-chip shop – which hardly topped the list as the most romantic setting.

We didn't get many opportunities to meet regularly. The Hilton Show Band became one of the most successful in Ireland, and Eleanor was constantly on the road with the band playing four or five nights a week. It wasn't until she decided to go solo and came to London that we got a chance to see more of each other. And it was while she was appearing at the Palladium that we announced our engagement.

We had originally intended to wait a while, but Eleanor's agent thought that the publicity would be helpful. When the telegrams of congratulation came flooding in, we didn't have the heart to tell all our friends that it was only really a 'trial run'. I never found out whether it boosted the box-office takings at the Palladium.

Eleanor had a contract with Decca and made seven records – she certainly wasn't after my money, since she was earning more than me at the time. But she didn't care for the life style of singing at clubs night after night and decided to give up her career when we married in January 1967.

It was a pity in some respects, for she undoubtedly had the talent to make the big-time. She assures me she has never regretted the decision to quit, though it would have been satisfying if she had made one hit record. But appearing at the Palladium was at least the equivalent of playing at Wembley. Now our three daughters, Siobhan, Ciára and Mairead, and son Patrick, keep Eleanor so busy that it must seem like playing extra time every day.

I love music. I sang in a school choir which won medals at more than one *feis* (an Irish festival of singing and dancing) and I even gave the occasional solo rendering. I wish I had the same confidence now, but the very thought terrifies me and not so long ago I turned down an offer to record a duet with Eleanor.

Now the only 'choir' I sing in comprises my club-mates. Both Spurs and Arsenal made recordings to mark Cup Final appearances, and more recently there was the Northern Ireland World Cup song.

These sessions used to present obvious problems for the recording director, trying to coax some kind of rhythm out of a bunch of self-conscious footballers. But then somebody had the bright idea of providing a crate of lagers to wet the whistle. It worked a treat – you'd be amazed the difference a couple of drinks can make.

2

MOVING TO SPURS

Bill McGarry sold me to Spurs in the summer of 1964 at the end of my one full season with Watford. By then I had played twice for Northern Ireland and there was speculation in the papers that I might be moving to a bigger club. But I was in no rush.

I was happy at Watford and got on well with the manager. I knew he was a tough disciplinarian, so I didn't give it a thought when I received a telegram from him telling me to report back for 'early training'. I just assumed that Watford were going to pull out all the stops in a bid to win promotion after the previous near miss.

McGarry was waiting to pick me up at London Airport and on the drive to the Watford ground he broke the news that I was to be transferred to Spurs. I don't know what he expected me to say, but my first question was, I confess, a typical one from a footballer: 'What's in it for me?'

Players were allowed to ask for a signing-on fee, and while I realized Spurs owed me nothing – and may have felt they were gambling in buying me – I thought I was due something from Watford who were making a profit of more than £20,000 in little more than a year. But McGarry didn't see it that way.

At Watford that afternoon I met Bill Nicholson for the very first time. I'd only seen him on television, but he was exactly as I'd imagined. He turned up carrying a little briefcase containing the transfer forms. He told me why Spurs wanted me, made it clear that there was a first-team place waiting if I came up to expectation and offered me wages of £38 a week. I said I was both flattered and delighted and that there was no club I would sooner join, but I pointed out I was earning almost as much at Watford as he was offering, and I surely rated something – from somebody.

It was deadlock. Nicholson was polite, but firm; there was nothing he could offer and he was disappointed because he had never been turned down before by any player he had tried to sign. We shook hands and I flew back to Ireland under the impression it was the end of the matter.

When I got home, the story broke that I had rejected a move to one of soccer's most famous clubs and I found myself under the hammer from several Irish pressmen. They seemed to think I had become too big for my boots by turning down such a golden opportunity. I suppose it did sound rather big-headed, yet I felt I was in the right.

I wasn't scared at the prospect of going into the First Division – far from it – but I was young and thought that if I was good enough I would get there in time. Meanwhile, I was prepared to play on at Watford.

I didn't anticipate hearing from Nicholson again, assuming he would look elsewhere for a goalkeeper. So I was surprised when I got another message from McGarry asking me to contact him. When I telephoned Watford it was to be told that Spurs were still keen and another meeting had been fixed. 'No thanks,' I replied. 'So far as I'm concerned there is nothing left to discuss. I'm having my close-season break – if you want to see me it will have to be in Ireland.'

It was a bit of a cheek, you don't have to tell me that, but the message must have got across. McGarry and Nicholson flew over and arranged to meet me at the Grand Central Hotel – now, unhappily, closed to the public – in the middle of Belfast.

The talking lasted a long time. McGarry made it clear that Watford needed the cash and that if I didn't move, I could expect to train all day and every day in the coming season. If I did, I would collect just £150 due under the existing system – which was called 'accrued share of benefit'.

I came to the conclusion that there was little point in staying where I wasn't wanted – and, anyway, the longer I spent in Nicholson's company the more impressed I became. So I signed for Spurs at an increased offer of £40 a week plus £5 for each first-team game.

My father had accompanied me to the Grand Central and I could sense he was amazed I even hesitated. He was earning about £11 a week and the money being discussed seemed a small fortune. But he urged me to ask for a ten-year contract. That added up to security which was far more important in his eyes. I didn't, of course, and if I had, I'm under no illusions what Nicholson would have said. Neither of us could have foreseen I would remain at White Hart Lane for the next 13 years.

Sometimes I wonder what would have happened to my career if Bill Nicholson had not been so persistent in pursuit of a raw kid. I'm only glad he did. I would not have liked to miss my time at Tottenham or the chance to play under such a great, and straight, manager.

So far as I'm concerned, Bill was something special. He was manager of Spurs during my first ten seasons at White Hart Lane and during that time there must have been more than a hundred players on the books. Not all of them got on well with Bill – but there wasn't one who didn't have the greatest respect for him.

That, above all else, was the quality he inspired from each of them, from the youngest apprentice to the most experienced first-teamer. Nobody ever cheated on Bill because he was always straight with the players. He was hard, he could even be unintentionally hurtful in his approach, but if he made a promise it was always kept.

In my eyes, and those of all the other professionals at the club, Bill Nicholson *was* Tottenham Hotspur. He kept the directors at a distance from us and seldom allowed them into the dressing room. If there was anything to be said to us, Bill was the man who said it.

He had few if any friends outside football: football in general, and Spurs in particular, was his life. Whether you called at the ground early in the morning or late at night, Bill was always there. It was the same story on a Sunday if you had to report for treatment.

It's said that when his elder daughter was married, Bill confided to somebody at the wedding reception that the realization had suddenly dawned upon him during the ceremony that he had not really seen his children grow up. I think that's rather sad, yet I'm sure it's true. Bill was married to Spurs as well as to his patient and always cheerful wife 'Darkie'.

Bill is a Yorkshireman who came down from Scarborough in pre-war days to sign for Spurs as a teenage full-back. Just after he had gained a regular first-team place, the war took a chunk out of his playing career. He served in the Army before returning to the club in 1946 and settling down in the new role of right-half. Bill was a fierce tackler, by all accounts, and I'm not surprised. Whatever he did for Spurs would be done one hundred per cent.

He played only once for England, scoring with his very first kick in a 5–2 victory over Portugal at Goodison Park. From conversations I've had with his contemporaries, the overwhelming opinion is that Bill was unlucky not to get far more caps. As it is, he spent most of his time as understudy to Billy Wright.

When he eventually hung up his boots, Bill became coach and then manager of Spurs and his record during 16 years in charge speaks for itself. The highlight was the League championship and FA Cup 'double' of 1960–61. He also won two more FA Cups, two League Cups, the European Cup-winners' Cup (the first ever success by a

British club in Europe back in 1963) and the UEFA Cup. It's a pity that the European Cup is missing from that roll of honour to give Bill a grand slam. He only had one crack at that, and Spurs were beaten by Benfica in the semi-finals.

Bill kept all the players on their toes and when he entered the dressing room in the morning – in those days he and his assistant, Eddie Baily, used to change with the rest of us before training – there was a general hush. Nobody clowned around when Bill was about, not even a joker like Jimmy Greaves. Nobody took liberties.

Bill was always the boss yet, unlike most managers, he never insisted on being called that by the players. On the contrary, the first time I met him – when he was negotiating my transfer from Watford – I naturally called him Mr Nicholson. 'You can forget the Mr, my name is Bill,' he promptly told me.

I was quite surprised. I was only a kid starting in the game and here was this legendary figure, who had achieved so much, treating me as an equal. I warmed to him on the spot.

Later I found he wasn't an easy man to know, and he took pains to avoid any of the players catching him with his defences down. Yet after an away game, if we were waiting at a railway station or an airport, Bill would often slip skipper Dave Mackay a tenner and tell him to buy the lads a drink. The money came out of his own pocket, but Bill never made a fuss about it. He rarely even joined us at the bar.

There were occasions, too, when I would take one of my daughters to the club if I was calling for a brief spot of treatment on a day off. Looking around to collect her, I would find her sitting in Bill's office loaded with apples and crisps. Bill always had time to chat with any of the players' children.

Oddly enough, the one time I saw Bill cry was on my first official duty for the club. It happened before the funeral of the great John White, who had been killed by lightning on a golf course on the day I was travelling from Ireland to report at Tottenham, for the first time, for pre-season training.

We all gathered at White Hart Lane before going on to the crematorium. Bill started to talk to us about John, who was only 24 when he died. He had been speaking for only a couple of minutes when he was so overcome that he excused himself and disappeared into the washroom to hide his tears. The players all said they had never seen Bill so distraught.

John's death ended another link with the 'double' team of three years earlier. Danny Blanchflower had retired, Terry Medwin's career had been finished by a broken leg, Bobby Smith and Terry Dyson had been transferred.

I had been signed to replace Scottish international Bill Brown, but in my first two seasons I was in and out of the team. I'm sure I was a disappointment to Bill Nicholson in those early days. He had been sufficiently impressed by my potential to buy me, but he didn't take into account that I was just 19, still learning my trade and had been playing in the Irish 'B' League only 18 months earlier. Bill expected me to make an instant impact.

Taking over from somebody as accomplished as Brown, who had given Spurs such excellent service, wasn't easy. I thought I was doing quite well, but there's no doubt I was still very raw. I was stopping shots, yet tending to push the ball away instead of holding it or turning it past the post. So we lost a goal or two from rebounds.

Bill didn't mess about – a bad game and you were out. And if your name wasn't on the team-sheet when it was pinned up on Friday, you knew it was up to you to do the business in the reserve side to try and earn a recall. It never occurred to you to knock on the manager's door and complain.

So far as I know, Bill only once showed a sign of losing faith in me. A story appeared in the papers that he had offered to swap me in part exchange for Millwall's Alex Stepney. To this day I don't know if it was true – I hadn't dared ask Bill – and it never went any further: Alex eventually went to Chelsea and then on to Manchester United to win European Cup and League championship medals.

If I had joined Spurs before the break-up of the 'double' team, life might have been simpler. But I arrived during a transitional period, when the side was no longer sweeping all before it and comparisons with the past were inevitable. Bill himself could never avoid them. He constantly judged Spurs by the highest standards and in many ways put pressure on the players that, frankly, we could have done without at the time.

His dream was always to recreate another fabulous team, and perhaps he became frustrated by failure to hit the jackpot again. When I look back at team photographs which span my Tottenham career, there's no doubt we had a succession of talented players on the books at different times. Somewhere along the line we ought to have won the First Division, but we were continually haunted by the spectre of the 'double' side.

There was one particular season when we seemed to find it impossible to win an away game. We were beating all-comers at White

Hart Lane, but once we set out on our travels – even if it was a short trip along the M1 – everything seemed to go wrong. It wasn't lack of fight, just one of those things which happens in soccer and starts to snowball. Before each away game we were reminded of our previous failures by the newspapers. Bill couldn't understand it at all. He even called a couple of team meetings to try and get at the root of the trouble, and that in itself almost added up to a crisis.

Bill rarely went in for team meetings, even before a match. His style was to sit next to a player in the dressing room and outline what he wanted from that individual. He would tell a full-back whether the opposing winger preferred to cut inside or go down the line. I'd get a breakdown on all the strikers – whether they liked to hit a ball with right foot or left, shoot from long range or try to get close, and whether they were inclined to volley the ball or let it drop to their feet before having a go. Bill even knew which opponents would elbow you in the ribs when a cross came over and those who would shirk a challenge. By the time he'd finished you knew what to expect, and when to expect it.

After a game Bill would come and sit beside you again, and tell you what you had done wrong – and what you hadn't done at all. If the team had won he tended to accept it as a right. He didn't throw much praise about.

He was seldom satisfied, and even after a 4–0 victory he would find fault. The longer-serving players used to tell how Bill had given the team a rollicking after winning 6–1 at West Ham. He wasn't kidding, either. Although it was, by all accounts, a boiling hot afternoon in August, he was furious that Spurs had eased up after taking a 6–0 lead and allowed West Ham to score.

My major criticism of Bill is that he overpraised opposing players before a game. He would get you thinking that you were about to meet a team of supermen. He'd build them up instead of occasionally telling us how good we were, and it wasn't always a shrewd tactic.

It didn't matter so much in the era of Dave Mackay and Jimmy Greaves, two players who would quietly smile to themselves and not say a word. They didn't suffer from an inferiority complex and some-times, after a match, they would toss out a throw-away remark that 'Mr Wonderful' on the other side must have had an off day. It was always for Bill's benefit and said within his hearing, but never addressed directly to him. But later, when Spurs didn't possess so many star players, I felt Bill made life harder for the lads and undermined their confidence when he praised the opposition to the skies.

All players are different, and Martin Chivers – who in terms of sheer ability was as good a centre-forward as I've played with or against – was one who used to get downhearted when Bill criticized him. Bill was always ramming Bobby Smith, centre-forward in the 'double' team, down Martin's throat. 'Bobby would have done this' or 'Bobby would have done that' he would tell Chivers after practically every match. Poor Martin would protest in vain, 'But I'm not Bobby Smith. If you wanted a Bobby Smith you should have signed one like him.'

Smith had been a physical player who liked to let opposing goal-keepers know he was around and who relished a no-holds battle with a rival centre-half. Chivers was a gentle giant. Despite his powerful build it simply wasn't in his nature to hustle and bustle, and it was unusual to see him lose his temper. He preferred to rely upon his skill.

Martin took a lot of verbal stick from Nicholson and Baily. They couldn't come to terms with his deceptively casual attitude, and were always attempting to get him to show an aggressive streak which wasn't in his make-up, especially after he suffered a terrible knee injury in a home game with Nottingham Forest which put him out of action for almost an entire season.

When Martin regained full fitness it took him a while to recapture his form, and that's when he needed encouragement. But Bill was hardly sympathetic and I recall him dropping Chivers for a First Division match at West Ham and telling Martin to sit in the stand and study the way Geoff Hurst played. 'That's what we want from you,' said Bill.

It seemed Martin couldn't win. Even when he scored over 40 goals for Spurs one season – an incredible total – Bill wasn't completely satisfied. Perhaps because, at his best, Martin made it all look so easy, Bill was convinced he should have got more goals. He admired Chivers, yet never really understood his man.

Because Bill had come up the hard way at Tottenham before the war, he also tended to be impatient with youngsters who were not prepared to serve their time and wait for a first-team place. He was an excellent judge of players and seldom made a mistake in assessing what they would eventually achieve, but he made a couple of errors by parting with future internationals Keith Weller and Graeme Souness at give-away fees.

Keith and Graeme both felt they were ready for the first team. Bill clearly thought they were trying to run before they could walk and instead of attempting to placate them he let them go. He had a mind of his own and there was no way that he would allow youngsters to dictate to him.

In the case of Weller, things came to a head when Keith reached 21, when players were then allowed to negotiate a new contract. Keith, although frustrated at his limited opportunities in the League side, was prepared to stay at White Hart Lane if he got the wage rise he wanted. Spurs said 'No' and Keith was transferred to Millwall at a bargain price. He emerged in his own right in the Second Division and then moved to Chelsea and Leicester, where he gained four England caps.

The crazy thing is that the difference between what Keith was asking Spurs, and what they offered him, was something like a fiver a week. That was in the summer of 1967 immediately after Spurs had won the FA Cup. It shows how times have changed.

If Bill was wrong about Weller, and on reflection I believe he would admit it, he could argue it was touch and go. But the decision to sell Souness to Middlesbrough for £45,000 a few years later was his biggest blunder.

Graeme was an unbelievable prospect – you could see that in training, for the skill was hanging out of him. He might have lacked pace – he does to this day, even though he has developed into a world-class footballer with Liverpool and Scotland – but he had wonderful ball control even as a kid.

Graeme knew he was head and shoulders above some of the players in the Spurs first team at the time, and he had an arrogance about him which is now part of his strength but was not exactly welcomed by Bill, Eddie and the rest of the coaching staff. He rubbed them up the wrong way.

I still find it incredible that Graeme didn't get into our First Division side, and I remember being put on the spot when Middlesbrough showed an interest in him. I received a call from Harold Shepherdson, their assistant manager, asking if I would recommend Souness. I had no option but to tell the truth and say 'without a shadow of a doubt' even though my instinct was to sound off-hand in the hope that Graeme would stay at Tottenham. 'He's arrogant, but it's justified,' I told Harold, 'because he is a hell of a player.'

One of the problems with Graeme, which speeded his departure from Spurs, was that he was often homesick for Edinburgh, so much so that he went absent and returned to Scotland on a couple of occasions, and Spurs had a lot of hassle getting him back to White Hart Lane. Bill never quite understood it, but I did. When you are a teenager and a long way from home, it's easy to become despondent. That's why I have always told kids at both Spurs and Arsenal to ask the manager to allow them to have a trip home if they are feeling lonely.

I'm talking from experience. I went through it myself when I left my family in Ireland – there were 11 of us at home at the time – to join Watford. Fortunately for me, Watford manager Bill McGarry knew the score and on at least three occasions he handed me an air ticket to Belfast and told me to take a long weekend with my folks. Bill McGarry was a dour character in the Nicholson mould, but I've never forgotten his thoughtfulness in that respect. It meant a great deal to me.

You have to be aware of his background, and the devotion he gave to Spurs, to understand the shock waves in the dressing room when Bill Nicholson left the club early in 1974–75. Admittedly, the team was having a rough spell but it never entered my head Spurs would let him go.

Bill and Eddie Baily had bent back our ears for as long as I could remember about the virtue of loyalty. But the Spurs board was short on loyalty to Bill and Eddie when the crunch came. They were both treated in a heartless and shabby manner.

I know that, officially, Bill 'resigned'. All I can say is that the directors didn't exactly resist his offer to go. And when you think of other managers at other clubs who have been granted testimonials for achieving a lot less, I gather Spurs weren't overgenerous with their pay-off to Bill and Eddie.

The pressure had been mounting on Bill for quite a while, and at one stage he was in favour of changing the set-up at White Hart Lane by bringing in his old 'double' skipper Danny Blanchflower as manager, with Republic of Ireland international Johnny Giles as player-coach. Bill would have delegated a lot of his responsibility and become general manager. The Spurs directors vetoed the idea – some of them, I'm told, felt Danny was too outspoken for their liking – and Bill must have been conscious of a loss of confidence in him.

Things came to a head in August 1974 when Spurs got off to their worst start to a season since 1912. After the fourth consecutive League defeat, Bill, who had served Spurs for 39 years, offered his resignation in the best interests of the club. Maybe it was an emotional reaction but, whatever Bill felt, the players thought it was the worst decision he ever made.

In many respects, the day Bill left was the beginning of the end for me at Tottenham. I was deeply shocked such a thing could happen. I remember my first thought on hearing the news was that if the club was relegated it served them right.

Dressing-room morale sunk to rock-bottom. Instead of worrying about the next match, the senior players were more concerned about having a whip-round to buy Bill a parting gift to show him how highly he was regarded by all of us. We gave it to him at a get-together at his house and a few of us were near to tears.

Bill, typically, used the occasion to give us a lecture that we must all give our wholehearted backing to the new manager, Terry Neill, and make sure Spurs didn't go down. I'm certain nobody in London was more delighted when we eventually saved ourselves from relegation by beating Leeds in the last match of the season.

It's probably difficult for anybody outside the club to appreciate just how much we respected Bill as a manager. I've often tried to analyse his strength, and I think it lay in the fact that he treated his players like men and expected them to act like men. He never ever fined a player.

When Keith Burkinshaw took over two years later, after Terry Neill had moved to Arsenal, he attempted to fine a number of players – me included – for reporting back ten minutes late one night while we were at a pre-season training camp in Germany. I told Keith that Bill never fined anybody, in all his time as boss, and Keith found it hard to believe.

To his eternal credit, Keith realized Bill had ruled by mutual respect and, knowing the players' deep feeling for him, he persuaded the directors to bring Bill back to White Hart Lane after his two years' exile at West Ham. That really delighted me.

Bill is now chief scout at Spurs and, because he stays in the background, I don't suppose any of the present players – apart from Steve Perryman – even imagine what a tremendous influence he once exerted upon club affairs.

3

GENTLEMAN JIM
AND OTHER SPURS CHARACTERS

It's just possible that, somewhere, there's a former First Division foot-baller who didn't like Jimmy Greaves as a person or admire him as a player – but, if so, I have yet to meet the fellow. I can honestly say I've never heard anybody say a bad word about 'Gentleman Jim'.

Yes, Jimmy is a gent, a smashing bloke – a truly great player who never let fame go to his head. In the six years we were together as Tottenham club-mates he was always one of the lads, never looking for special treatment despite his remarkable talent.

When he packed up playing – which he did at least five seasons too soon – and the rumours filtered back to White Hart Lane that he was hitting the bottle, we were all horrified. When the news was confirmed (and Jimmy has since recorded in detail how bad things became) everybody who knew him had nothing but sympathy.

All the Spurs players knew Jimmy liked his half of bitter, yet the only occasion I ever saw him take anything stronger was in an airport before we were leaving for a European tie or a tour game. Jimmy hated flying in his Spurs days and liked a brandy or two before take-off, though, ironically, he conquered his fear of aeroplanes before he hung up his boots.

Whatever the reasons for the long 'lost weekend' in Jimmy's life, his character triumphed in the end and he kicked the drinking habit. That gave me more pleasure than winning my first FA Cup final – which, as it happens, I did in the same team as Jimmy in 1967. Now he has carved a new career as a TV analyst and newspaper columnist. However successful he may become in that sphere, he can hardly match his fabulous achievements on a football pitch.

I was still a novice, despite having played two internationals for Northern Ireland, when I joined Spurs in 1964 and first met the maestro. He was only 24 himself, but he'd been a headliner since the age of 17 and by that time had already scored more than 200 First Division goals. I found it hard to believe that such an exceptional player, accepted as genuine world-class, could be so modest. And I was eternally grateful for the encouragement he gave me during my first season or so at Tottenham.

If I had a poor game, and was conscious of other people muttering about my mistakes, Jimmy was always the first to offer reassurance. He would put an arm round my shoulder and say 'Forget it, we all have our bad 'uns;' and he would add, 'You are going to be the best, just give it time.' I don't kid myself that Jimmy really thought I had a golden future in the game. I think he would have acted exactly the same way to anybody. It's the way he's made.

There's probably a higher percentage of nice guys in footballing circles than most outsiders would believe, considering all they read, but I have never met one who was more popular with his team-mates than Jimmy. Whereas George Best tended to be a loner when the mood grabbed him, Jimmy was always the life and soul of any get-together. He loved a sing-song, especially if it gave him the chance to render a chorus or two of his theme song, 'Maybe it's because I'm a Londoner'.

Thousands upon thousands of words have been written about Jimmy's footballing ability, and even the most lyrical are not an exaggeration. He really was 'magic' before that word became part of soccer's vocabulary. He was a scorer of memorable goals, but that was only part of his skill.

Jimmy could go past defenders as if they weren't there, yet one of his qualities which wasn't fully appreciated was his courage. Jimmy didn't get involved in running battles, but I never saw him 'bottle' a tackle. He was as brave as anybody where it mattered, in the opposition's penalty area.

Some people used to claim he was a 'moocher', who let those around him do the hard work while he lurked upfield waiting to sneak a goal. That myth was probably born because he could be almost unseen for 85 minutes, then create a chance out of thin air to snatch a winner. But, while unnoticed from the terraces, you can be sure opponents were ever-conscious Jimmy was around. He possessed fantastic pace, so that he was uncatchable once he was on the goal side of any marker, and could control a pass driven at him at 80 mph, kill the ball dead and beat an opponent all in a split second if he was on form.

Alan Gilzean, another class striker who formed a lethal partnership with Greaves, once admitted to me that during the first half-dozen games he played for Spurs he thought Jimmy was a lucky player. Alan, like the rest of us, just couldn't believe that Jimmy could so often be in the right place at exactly the right moment to score. But the longer they were together the more Alan's admiration for Jimmy grew. Alan didn't care for the physical stuff, yet he would willingly have run through a brick wall for Jimmy. That was the kind of effect he had on all his mates.

Everything Jimmy did was economical and clinical. Ask him to keep the ball up 30 or 40 times in a training session, and – unlike many lesser players – he couldn't do it. He never mastered that skill because it wasn't needed in a game.

He didn't care too much for training, and regarded running a dozen laps round a track as an utter waste of time. But such was his competitive spirit that if a test was introduced during training, perhaps for a small prize, then nine times out of ten there would be only one winner: J. Greaves, Esq.

I used to marvel at his ability in kick-about games in the Spurs gymnasium, with goals measuring 6ft by 4ft and so many players taking part you could hardly move without treading on somebody's toes. Even in such crowded conditions, Jimmy would find space where none seemed to exist and such was his uncanny goal-sense he would always be among the scorers. He was greased lightning.

But I stopped him once, the hard way, in a gym encounter. I was playing out of goal on the opposite side and went to tackle Jimmy. He promptly sold me a dummy, but I wasn't bright enough to buy it – and we crashed together with an unmerciful crack of heads. I looked up at Jimmy and saw him streaming with blood, then I felt hot blood running down my face.

It was a Friday morning and, fortunately, the club doctor was on the premises and led us both to the dressing room to be stitched. Through a haze I heard Jimmy tell the doc, 'Look after Pat first, he's more important for tomorrow.' That must rate as the biggest compliment I've ever been paid. I finished with six stitches and went home concussed, and both Jimmy and I still had headaches when we turned out against Stoke the following afternoon.

One thing's for sure, I wouldn't have got so close to Jimmy in a real game. When he was clear with only a goalkeeper to beat the outcome was as near to inevitable as anything can be.

We had been together at Tottenham just three months when I got a first-hand example of the accuracy of Jimmy's finishing powers. It was my first game against England, at Windsor Park, Belfast, and a red-letter day for me. At least it should have been, but Jimmy ruined it with a hat-trick before half-time. I wasn't looking forward to the second half, I can tell you, but – much to my relief – the dreaded

Greaves didn't strike again and an Irish revival meant that England ended hanging on for a 4–3 victory.

Jimmy's finest goal? Impossible to answer that question, because he scored so many that live in the memory. But few of them were more spectacular than one against Aston Villa when he was ten yards out with his back to goal when the ball dropped. Most players of Jimmy's size would have been pleased to head it. He executed a text-book scissors kick to score with an overhead shot. The crowd were as stunned as the players and there was a moment's silence before they burst into wild applause.

If I had to choose his most valuable goal for Spurs, at least in my time, it was another spectacular effort which helped us to a 2–1 victory over Nottingham Forest in the 1967 FA Cup semi-final. Forest were chasing the League and FA Cup double that season – they finished with neither, coming second to Manchester United in the First Division – and started favourites to beat Spurs. But they were victims of the remarkable Greaves.

I have stressed Jimmy's popularity with his team-mates, but it extended far beyond the dressing room. The fans thought the world of him, because he was never too busy to sign his autograph or have a chat with them. The same applied to the press. Jimmy didn't need publicity, his exploits on the field earned it for him automatically, yet he was noted among journalists for his readiness to have a word – and a wisecrack – whenever he was approached. He really was a model professional and an object lesson to any young player.

His most bitter disappointment was when Sir Alf Ramsey left him out of the England team which defeated West Germany 4–2 in extra time in the 1966 World Cup final. Jimmy missed the quarter-final against Argentina through injury and Geoff Hurst came in as replacement and scored the only goal of the game.

Greaves still wasn't fit for the semi-final with Portugal which England won 2–1, and the England manager decided to keep the same side for the final. It must have been the toughest decision anybody has been called upon to make, and since Hurst earned soccer immortality with a Wembley hat-trick it's got to be said the choice was right. But, somehow, it still seems an injustice that Jimmy missed out.

Altogether it ended a season, 1965–66, that wasn't the luckiest for Jimmy. He was out of the Spurs side for several months with hepatitis, an illness which is noted for its after-effects. Other sportsmen who have been afflicted by it have said it took them a year or more to regain full fitness, so Jimmy probably came back too soon, partly because of his importance to Spurs and partly because of the World Cup looming up. He still got among the goals – four in one England game in Norway – but, not surprisingly, found it difficult consistently to reproduce his peak form.

Jimmy seldom talked about his feelings in having to watch the World Cup final, instead of playing in it, but I got the impression that it was a long time before he was able to shrug off the despair that must have bitten into him so deeply.

It was hardly comparable when Bill Nicholson made his decision to drop Jimmy, along with several other regular first-teamers, from the Spurs side for a third round FA Cup replay against Crystal Palace at Selhurst Park in January 1970. But although everybody at White Hart Lane thought it was only a temporary measure at the time, it proved to be virtually the end of Jimmy's career with Spurs.

We lost the replay 1–0, but Jimmy wasn't recalled. The odd hint began to appear in the papers that Spurs would allow him to leave, if they could negotiate a suitable exchange deal, but few of the other players at the club believed Bill Nicholson would let Jimmy go. He was still without a peer as a goal-getter, and his form in practice matches was as sharp as it had ever been.

In March of that year the unthinkable happened. On deadline day Jimmy left Spurs for West Ham, and what's more he went in part-exchange for Martin Peters. The dressing room was like a morgue when we learned the news. It was the chance to get Peters, a player of star quality, which tempted manager Nicholson and Martin certainly proved a great acquisition for the club. Yet we all wished there had been some other way to sign Martin.

There is no doubt in my mind that Spurs made a mistake in parting with Jimmy, and that he could easily have given the club another five years' service. The transfer did him no great favours, either, for Jimmy spent less than 18 months at West Ham and failed to enhance his reputation at Upton Park.

He started well enough with a couple of goals in his opening game, a runaway victory over Manchester City at Maine Road, but most West Ham fans will tell you that Jimmy never clicked at Upton Park. It is perhaps a back-handed compliment that Jimmy's failure at West Ham still brought him an average of a goal every three games despite the fact that in several of them he was confined to a midfield role.

Any striker who totals 14 goals in 42 League games during a season is judged to have done reasonably well, but Jimmy of course was measured by his own high standards – and with both Spurs and his first club, Chelsea, he scored at a rate of two goals every three League matches.

When he packed up, at the ridiculously early age of 31, he was credited with 357 First Division goals. It's a First Division record, and a superman will have to appear on the scene if it is ever to be broken. The tragedy, and I don't think that is too strong a word, is that Jimmy could have had so many more. I reckon he could have added another hundred if he'd remained at White Hart Lane.

One of his West Ham goals came in a 2–2 draw at Tottenham on the opening day of 1970–71. It was Jimmy's return to the ground where he had been such an idol and, although none of us suspected it at the time, it was to be his last appearance there in a League match.

It was a typical Greaves goal. He had hardly had a kick all afternoon when West Ham forced a corner on the left. When the ball came over the goalmouth was crowded yet, suddenly, a big hole seemed to open up and there was Jimmy. As always he had found space where none seemed to exist, and I hardly saw his shot as it flew into the net way beyond my reach.

I can remember the goal vividly and my strange mixed feelings about it. Spurs had lost a home point, yet deep down I was pleased for Jimmy that he had scored on his White Hart Lane home-coming.

The following summer he announced his retirement from League football. Jimmy couldn't be persuaded to change his mind, and it was years later before he came to regret his premature decision.

At first he insisted he enjoyed turning out each Saturday for his works' team on local parks' pitches, a dreadful waste for he was being watched by a handful of onlookers when he should have been entertaining thousands. Subsequently, in his mid to late thirties, he played in senior non-League football with several clubs including Barnet.

Jimmy could have gone on for donkey's years in League football with a good team, and he underlined that point when he played at White Hart Lane in several testimonial matches. He took part in mine, five years after he had quit, and starred in a game against Arsenal that was fought with all the tension of a First Division fixture. He not only scored, but made some of the players around him look like cart-horses by comparison.

The first of the testimonials was for Jimmy himself, marking a change in policy by Spurs who had previously refused to sanction such games. That was against crack Dutch club Feyenoord and some indication of the regard in which Jimmy was held by the fans was reflected by an attendance of 45,000.

I was thrilled he got such a good crowd although I was sad I was unable to play. I was on duty with Northern Ireland, and Barry Daines took my place in the Spurs team.

It seemed only right that Jimmy was able to cash in to some extent, for by modern standards he never received high wages. At West Ham, and probably in his final season with Spurs, he got £100 a week. That's peanuts today, of course, and it wasn't so wonderful then when you recall that Fulham had made Johnny Haynes the very first £100-a-week British footballer immediately the maximum-wage restriction was lifted back in 1962.

Because I was unable to take part in Jimmy's testimonial game, I was slightly embarrassed about asking him to play in mine in November 1976. He certainly didn't owe me anything; any debt was loaded the other way. So I was thrilled when I got a call from one of his close friends to let me know that Jimmy would like to play in my game if a place could be found for him. It took me about five seconds to accept the offer.

I wanted him to play not because his presence would be an extra crowd-puller, but simply so that in years to come – when I had retired – I could say Jimmy Greaves had played in my match. Somehow it wouldn't have been complete without him.

I recall a goal he got that night, not because it was a masterpiece but because it bore the Greaves hallmark with the ball skimming a post as it entered the net. That was one of Jimmy's assets: he was so accurate that he could place a ball within inches of a post – and out of a goalkeeper's reach – when other players would have been content to get in any kind of shot.

I lost count of the times I saw a keeper attempt to force Jimmy to shoot in a certain direction by leaving him space on one side of the goal. It was a ploy which seldom worked, for the usual outcome was that Jimmy would score on the 'wrong' side through the narrowest of gaps.

His timing was so perfect that Jimmy could have excelled at most sports and, in the summer of 1970, he took part in a hazardous World Cup motor rally as co-driver to Tony Ford. The route passed through much of South America before ending in Mexico City to coincide with the World Cup kick-off.

Jimmy was an excellent driver and loved fast cars, yet he wasn't a 'car nut' who was constantly talking about driving or motor racing. When he got the invitation, via the Ford motor company, it was simply the kind of challenge he could not resist.

It was a tough endurance test, and Jimmy practised for months in advance to prepare himself for the Rally. Yet even he was a bit shaken by the conditions and it was that experience which cured his fear of flying.

When Jimmy and Tony Ford completed the course and arrived in Mexico City he got a shock to learn that his pal Bobby Moore, the England skipper, was living in the British Embassy for a few days. It was a form of protection for Bobby after he had been falsely accused by a jeweller in the Colombian capital of Bogota of participating, with other England players, in the theft of a bracelet.

Nobody was allowed to visit Bobby at the embassy, but that didn't deter Jimmy who scaled a wall and climbed over a roof in order to see his mate. Once again he had found the gap in a defensive system.

Jimmy Greaves was one of the most influential people to help shape my career with Spurs, and another was Dave Mackay – a born leader as well as a great footballer. I have played under some fine captains, Alan Mullery being one of them, yet it's no reflection on any of the others when I rate Mackay the best of the lot.

He never shirked a challenge in his life and hated to see any player 'bottle' a tackle, even if he was on the other side. Dave just couldn't understand it, because it was foreign to his own nature. Not that many Spurs players were guilty of such evasive action if he was around. I knew a few who would jump out of a tackle, but once Dave was at their side they seemed to forget their own fear and draw strength from his presence.

Dave inspired his own team-mates and intimidated opponents, many of whom went strangely quiet after being on the receiving end of a Mackay blockbuster. He believed football was a man's game and expected no favours on the field, yet he never set out to hurt anybody and had no time for a player who went 'over the top' with a tackle. Not that many tried it on him.

Because of the strength of his tackling, Dave had a reputation as a hard man which I felt caused him to get less than the credit he deserved for his skills. And he was one of the most skilful players I've seen. Right foot, left foot, fierce volley or cunning lob, Dave had the lot – you name it and he could do it. He was such a talented all-round performer he could have played in any position and been a success. Yes, even in goal.

Dave was at Tottenham five years before I arrived, and was a key man when Spurs became the first club this century to achieve the

League championship and FA Cup double. I'm told he turned in fabulous performances week after week in that run of success. I have also been assured that by the time I joined Spurs he was past his peak, and I have to accept that is probably true. All I can say is that the mind boggles at what he must have been like if what I saw was not his best.

Dave had broken his leg at Old Trafford, in a European Cup-winners' tie against Manchester United midway through the previous season, and was battling to regain his fitness when I first met him. He played in pre-season friendly games in Glasgow and Rotterdam, but still carried a slight limp.

When the League campaign got under way, Dave was finding the going difficult and it was decided he needed a couple of reserve outings. In one of them, against Shrewsbury at White Hart Lane, he broke the same leg a second time.

That afternoon I was playing for the first team at Upton Park, and we lost 3–2. When we got back to the dressing room and heard what had happened to Dave, the result was forgotten in the general gloom of the skipper's set-back. Bill Nicholson was absolutely choked – like the rest of us he must have felt it was the end of a great career.

We should have known better. Dave was always a winner and he wasn't going to be beaten, even by a twice-broken leg which would have finished most players. His come-back was so complete that three seasons later he captained Spurs to victory over Chelsea in the FA Cup final at Wembley.

Dave was a strange mixture. He might not thank me for revealing the fact, but he has a heart of gold. He'd give his last penny to a pal in trouble. And if any of the lads asked to borrow his car, a Jaguar, he'd toss them the keys without a second thought. Yet in any competition he wanted to come out on top, and usually did. I used to play golf with Dave, Alan Gilzean and Mike England and he was never beaten until the very last hole. If he couldn't beat you, he'd try and talk you out of it.

Five-a-side training matches turned into a war when Dave was involved. If I wasn't playing myself, I could always hear Dave roaring from a distance of 50 yards as he urged his team on. But he was most impressive at shooting practice. He would have another player crossing the ball from the wing, and whatever height or angle it reached him Dave could fire in a telling volley. He was a human conveyor belt.

It was a shock when, shortly before the start of the 1968–69 season,

Dave left Spurs for Derby. We all had doubts about the wisdom of allowing him to go.

There had been talk that Dave might return to his former Scottish club, Hearts, who were surely robbed when they sold him to Spurs nine years earlier for a mere £30,000, but when we turned up for training one morning we spotted Brian Clough. Clough gets players to visit him these days when he is interested in signing them, but on this occasion he had travelled to see Dave – and I'm sure he never regretted the journey.

Derby had ended the previous season fighting against relegation from the Second Division. With Dave in the team they romped away with the championship, which came as no surprise to any of the Spurs players. We all knew the Derby lads would play above themselves with Dave driving them on.

He spent the best part of a couple of seasons with Derby in the First Division, before leaving to become player-manager of Swindon Town. When he played against Spurs I used to marvel that he still possessed all his old ability to control a game. At times it seemed impossible to get past him. Dave Mackay still looked something special, and I used to wish he was playing for us.

Two other former footballers whom I admired for the strength of their character are the brothers Cyril and Peter Knowles. Both retired prematurely as players, for very different reasons.

Cyril was my closest friend at White Hart Lane, for we were both signed by Spurs in the summer of 1964 and shared the same digs until I married three years later. He was a cheerful fellow, always bubbling with the sheer joy of life and good for a laugh. He had all the attributes of an outstanding full-back and I rated him unlucky to gain only four England caps.

Cyril was forced to pack up through injury at the age of 30, and though he had a good career there's no doubt in my mind that he could have continued playing at the top for several more years but for knee trouble. During his time with Tottenham he was an automatic choice for the first team, totalling 400 First Division games – so Bill Nicholson got full value for the £45,000 he paid Middlesbrough for Cyril.

Now Cyril is back with Middlesbrough, as a coach, and we still keep in touch regularly. Cyril and his wife Betty have rebuilt their life after the death of their young son Jonathan in tragic circumstances. It happened just when Cyril's playing career was coming to an end, and some people would have gone completely to pieces. Thank God, they came through the ordeal.

I met Cyril's kid brother Peter only a few times, when I spent a weekend with their parents at their Yorkshire home in Fitzwilliam. Peter was then making his mark in the Wolves team, and it was obvious that he was a player of exceptional ability.

He was an England youth international, a prolific scorer as a teenager who continued to get goals regularly in the First Division. Peter soon won a place in the Under-23 side, and it seemed inevitable that he would eventually get into the full England side. There wasn't a better prospect around, and he had that touch of arrogance about his play which is often the hallmark of a star forward.

Then, at the age of 24 with the soccer world at his feet, Peter suddenly announced he was giving up professional football to preach the gospel as a Jehovah's Witness.

The cynical reaction in the Spurs dressing room when the news hit the sports pages must have been echoed throughout the game. Peter was such an extrovert that nobody believed it. 'He'll be back within six months,' we all said – especially Cyril. But Peter never did come back, turning away from the bright lights and the ever-increasing wage packets soccer had to offer.

I hold up my hands to him for having the courage of his convictions, for his action made him unique in my experience. We have all read stories of well known footballers who, in a moment of depression, have said they would not play again. But that kind of mood soon passes with the realization that, for the majority, it would be impossible to earn comparable money outside the game. Perhaps that is why Wolves kept Peter's registration for years – in the belief that he would eventually have second thoughts. Yet not even an occasional appearance in a testimonial match, when his skill remained apparent even though he was a bit overweight, tempted him to return.

I must admit the thought crossed my mind that Peter might have been able to do more for the cause and image of the Jehovah's Witnesses had he continued playing and remained in the limelight. Chelsea's Bobby Tambling, who shared the same faith, did so and was widely regarded as a credit to the game and his religion. But Peter felt the two things were worlds apart, so he made his choice and stuck to it.

I am fortunate to have been associated with a lot of nice people during my career, and a trainer for whom I have a great deal of affection is

Cecil Poynton of Spurs. I suppose 'dour' would be the most accurate description of Cecil, but he still enjoyed a laugh with the lads.

Cecil played for Spurs in the twenties and must have been at least 60 when I arrived at White Hart Lane – though he looked 15 years younger. And when he used to lead us on pre-season road walks he lasted the pace as well as any of the players.

Even if not as gifted as the late Bobby McGregor, the finest trainer in the game, there's no doubt Cecil was good at his job; and he was certainly willing. He would spend hours at a time on an injured player to get him fit for the next match, and was so dedicated that he often got home late for his evening meal.

Like most former players who become trainers – and Pat Molloy at Watford was another great old-timer – Cecil took considerable personal pride in his own fitness. And he could be merciless on any player whom he felt was exaggerating an injury and spending too much time in the treatment room.

Cecil shared with manager Bill Nicholson a tendency to compare current players unfavourably with those who had figured in earlier Spurs sides. He liked to tell stories about some of the characters who had worn a Tottenham shirt, and he had an unbelievable memory when it came to recounting match incidents of 25 or 30 years ago. But he could never remember where he had left his keys 20 minutes before.

There was one occasion when he was leaving the ground at the end of the day and discovered, to his horror, that his car was missing from the White Hart Lane forecourt. He wasn't amused, for Cecil always kept his car in immaculate condition, and feared it might be damaged if – as he first suspected – some of the players had moved it as a joke.

When investigation revealed it wasn't a prank, Cecil duly reported the 'theft' to the local police and caught a bus home in a very black mood. Only then did he suddenly recall that he had visited the chemist earlier in the day, and, sure enough, he found the car parked outside. Cecil had walked back to the ground from the chemist's shop, a few streets away – completely forgetting he had driven there in the first place. It took him ages to live that episode down. Afterwards, when anything went missing, the players always suggested that Cecil should have a look outside the chemist's.

His assistant was Johnny Wallis, another diamond of a bloke, who seemed to spend his entire life at the club. Johnny loved Spurs and in his time had fulfilled just about every back-room job. He looked after the apprentice professionals, assigning them to their daily tasks, and acted in turn as trainer of the youth team, reserves and first team.

He later became the kit man, a job which takes up almost every hour of the day. Just imagine cleaning countless pairs of boots after each training session and having them spick and span for the following morning, and ensuring that boots and the rest of the kit are in perfect condition for every game – home or away, in this country or abroad.

Arsenal have the equivalent of Johnny Wallis in Tony Donnolly, another hard-working, cheerful fellow who is very popular with the players. Tony is a member of the 'Irish Mafia' at Highbury, which at one period outnumbered the English and Scots on first-team trips.

People like Johnny and Tony are probably only paid buttons, but they are the backbone of any club because they enjoy their work. They realize that, although never in the limelight, their efforts are really appreciated by the players.

When Bill Nicholson was manager, Spurs was blessed with a loyal staff and was a 'homely' club at all levels. Bill's secretary Mrs Wallace was a Mum to all the players, and Mrs Bick on the switchboard was just as helpful. Yet the directors were more remote than those of Arsenal, who go out of their way to make the players feel important.

In my early days at Tottenham I felt that the directors took the supporters for granted, and they certainly put up a barrier to those who could afford to travel all over the country – and abroad – and stay at the same hotels as the official Spurs party.

There were five or six of them, and the best known was Morris Keston who was a good friend of all the players. He's a life-long Spurs fan and you knew something remarkable must have happened if Morris missed a match.

He once went to Cairo to see Spurs play a friendly game with an Egyptian side at a time when relations between Israel and Egypt were more than slightly strained. Although Jewish, Morris stated his religion as Church of England on the entry visa in order to get to Cairo.

But he wasn't any more welcome there than when he turned up on the Friday night in Manchester before Spurs played at Maine Road and Old Trafford. The directors mistakenly regarded him as a hanger-on when nothing could have been further from the truth, since Morris took great pains to stay in the background.

The players never understood that attitude. We were all aware how much Morris contributed to any testimonial function for footballers with other clubs as well as Spurs. At auctions he was always the first to buy a shirt, or an international cap or some other item of gear he didn't really need to support the player involved. Most of all, he turned up at every game even when Spurs were struggling, so there was never any question that he was just a fair-weather fan. You get a lot of those who soon melt away when things are going badly.

Now, happily, Morris is on friendly terms with the present Spurs directors. It's just a pity the breakthrough took so long.

4

'WE'VE DECIDED TO LET YOU GO'

I spent 13 seasons with Spurs and I shall always have a lasting affection for the club. So it still upsets me to reflect that my stay at White Hart Lane did not have the happiest of endings. I didn't leave after any blazing row, but there was certainly a sour note to my departure.

Those seasons at Tottenham were, in the main, successful. Spurs won the FA Cup in 1967, the League Cup in 1971 and 1973, the UEFA Cup in 1972 as well as reaching the UEFA Cup final again two years later when we were beaten by Feyenoord of Holland. In my first ten seasons with the club we twice finished in third place in the First Division table and never dropped below the half-way mark.

I played a record number of League games for Spurs, overhauling the previous best by Ted Ditchburn, although after I left White Hart Lane my total was passed by my good friend Steve Perryman. Spurs even made a profit on me. I had been signed from Watford for £27,500 in the summer of 1964 and was sold to Arsenal for £45,000 in August 1977.

Yet what bothers me is that many Spurs fans have been led to believe that I was responsible for the break when it came; that I put the pressure on Spurs to let me leave for a number of reasons.

It has been said that I wanted to go because Spurs had been relegated at the close of the previous season and that I refused to play in the Second Division. Not true.

It was hinted I had made up my mind to be on my way once I'd had a testimonial match the previous November so that I could make a financial killing elsewhere. Not true.

It was claimed by people in the 'know' that the Spurs directors felt I was greedy and that I had asked for a lump sum, or a new contract with sky-high wages, in order to stay at Tottenham. Not true.

I was happy to stay and try to help Spurs get back into the First Division, and at no time did I ask for a transfer.

Nobody was more shocked than I was when Spurs decided it was time for me to go. And the reason was simply that manager Keith Burkinshaw, and the directors, had come to the conclusion that the club's interests would be better served with Barry Daines – who was six years younger – as first-team goalkeeper.

Barry had been my understudy for ages and had played in 19 League games during the relegation season when I was injured. He had shaped well and Keith felt that Daines was ready for a permanent take-over, and that I was surplus to requirements.

Fair enough. I'm sure it was an honest decision. What wasn't fair was that nobody at Tottenham came out and put their cards on the table with an explanation for the supporters. It was inferred that I had created the situation.

I have nothing against Keith. He backed his judgment and did what he regarded was right for Spurs. He's a straight enough bloke, so why didn't he come out with a statement of the facts? It would have avoided a great deal of misunderstanding, for so many fans still think the transfer was down to me. It would certainly have saved me count-less explanations to Spurs fans, convinced that I had deserted the club and crossed over to the 'enemy' at Highbury.

I understood Keith's reasoning, though I totally disagreed with it. I knew that at 32 I was far from over the hill, and I'm gratified that I proved the point with Arsenal.

If Keith had made public what he thought, instead of keeping silent, he would have got the credit if I had failed at Arsenal. Instead, in the next four years he took a lot of criticism which didn't die down until he paid £300,000 to Liverpool for Ray Clemence. I had to smile when that deal went through because Ray was 33 when he arrived at White Hart Lane, a year older than I was when I left.

Age undoubtedly influenced the Spurs directors to give the go-ahead to my transfer, and for more than the obvious reason that I was 32 and they couldn't be sure how long I would last. At that time the Professional Footballers' Association were negotiating with the Foot-ball League and the Football Association to introduce a clause in contracts to the effect that a player with more than five years' service with a club would be given a free transfer at the end of his contract if 33 or older. So Spurs, knowing I would be able to walk out in another year if I so decided, must have felt it was worth their while getting what they could.

Perhaps the build-up to my Spurs farewell began the previous summer, before the 1976–77 season which was to end in relegation and see Spurs lose their First Division status after an unbroken run of 27 years.

Terry Neill had joined Arsenal after two years as Spurs manager, a move which sparked off a good deal of ill-feeling and was greatly resented in the Tottenham board-room. The directors took it badly, thinking that Terry, by his switch, had intimated that the Arsenal job was better than being Spurs' boss; that, if you like, Arsenal were a bigger club.

During his two seasons in charge, Spurs had mixed fortunes. In Terry's first season – he didn't arrive from Hull until after we had played a few games and were rock bottom of the table – Spurs scraped clear of relegation by winning our last game 4–2 at home to Leeds. But the next season there was a steady improvement and we finished in ninth position.

It looked as if he had left a useful team for his successor, and Spurs advertised for a new manager in that summer of 1976. There was considerable speculation about who would get the job and Keith Burkinshaw, who had been at White Hart Lane for 12 months as first-team coach after being sacked by Newcastle, was among the applicants.

He wasn't tipped as one of the favourites and, to be honest, I didn't think Keith was the man Spurs needed at the time. He was a useful coach, but I didn't feel he had the necessary experience to lift the side into a position where we would be challenging for the championship. And, after a lean spell, I wanted to see Spurs back among the honours and I thought a big-name manager would persuade the directors to spend on new players.

Everybody at the club liked Keith, and most of the other players thought he deserved the chance to see what he could do. So a meeting was called, a vote was taken to back Burkinshaw and skipper Steve Perryman was delegated to convey the dressing-room feeling to the directors the following day.

Steve asked to see chairman Sidney Wale, who left a board meeting to listen to the players' view that Keith should be considered for the manager's job. Mr Wale must have been delighted, for a few minutes earlier, I'm told, the directors had decided to appoint Keith.

By sheer coincidence I wasn't at the meeting and therefore took no part in the vote. I don't know to this day whether Keith is aware of that fact, but there was no sinister reason for my absence. I missed the meeting because I had a prior appointment with Mr Wale.

In the aftermath of Terry Neill's departure, Mr Wale had said, in an effort to restore the club's old homely atmosphere, that he was always ready to see any of the players if they needed any help of any kind. I took him up on his invitation because I was moving house and had asked the club for a £10,000 loan to bridge the gap between the house I was selling and the new one. Frankly, I thought it would be a formality since I would pay the club interest at the usual bank rate. And, anyway, I only wanted the cash until my testimonial game was staged a few months later.

It was a shock when I was told that wealthy Spurs couldn't find £10,000 because the club had already budgeted for that year. I couldn't believe it. I didn't think I was asking a big favour with my testimonial coming up, especially as I had made things easy for Spurs by delaying my testimonial for a year so that Alan Gilzean – who had signed six months after me – could get in first because he was soon to leave White Hart Lane.

Maybe I didn't realize it then, but it was a hint that I was not as popular with the directors as I had assumed after 12 years' service. I was to get further evidence before I finally departed.

There's no denying I was shaken by Mr Wale's refusal, and unconvinced by his reasons. But I simply turned elsewhere and took out a mortgage to complete the purchase of the new house.

When the season kicked off I had a groin injury and missed the opening five League games, Daines deputizing, and Spurs broke even in that spell with five points – recovering after losing the two opening fixtures, away to Ipswich and at home to Newcastle.

It looked like being an average kind of season and I went into the side as soon as I was fit. But results were poor in the next four or five months and it became obvious that we were going to have a struggle to stay up.

I was playing reasonably well, but I was carrying an ankle injury which I just couldn't shake off. I was able to train full out and didn't feel the ankle was a handicap, except that I was unable to take goal-kicks.

I thought originally the injury was something I would shake off in a couple of games, but it persisted. I didn't see it as a problem, but it became one when other players complained about having to take my goal-kicks. They felt it prevented them moving upfield to play opponents offside and was encouraging opposing forwards to push up on our defenders and into our penalty area.

It had happened before, without comment, but I suppose that when results go badly it's only natural that everybody tries to find explanations. But I admit I thought it strange, for every goalkeeper has periods when he is restricted in some way. You aren't a hundred per cent fit every time you step on to the field. In fact, I remember former England keeper Gordon West – when he was at Everton – going almost through a season without being able to take goal-kicks. He kept his place because of his other assets.

My injury had now become a problem and I felt that if people didn't want me to play while it lasted there was no point in carrying on. Eventually I dropped out of the team, hoping the rest would prove a cure. It didn't work. Our physio Mick Varney tried all kinds of treatment without effect, and in the end he went with me when I tried acupuncture to try and find a solution.

I had missed a dozen League games. Daines was in the side and wasn't doing badly, but results hadn't improved and relegation was beginning to look a definite possibility instead of just a threat. So Keith began to think about bringing me back.

He asked me to come to the gym while he put me through a strenuous training session. He said 'let's give the ankle a go' and, although it was giving me a lot of pain whenever I kicked the ball, I gritted my teeth and carried on until he was satisfied.

Spurs had five League games left when I was recalled, and we knew we probably needed eight points to avoid the drop. It was beyond us. Although we got a goalless draw at Stoke and then beat Villa 3–1 at White Hart Lane, our fate was sealed at Maine Road when Manchester City outplayed us to win 5–0. Peter Barnes was right on song that afternoon, giving our defence a run-around and climaxing his display with a spectacular goal.

Our fate was already sealed when we played our last match of the season against Leicester City at White Hart Lane, and a 2–0 victory did nothing to ease the pain of going down. The fans put on a wonderful show of loyalty that afternoon. More than 26,000 turned up and they not only cheered every kick, but swarmed on to the pitch after the final whistle and called for the team to make an appearance. It was a trifle eerie in the circumstances, for I expected them to go home quietly instead of kicking up the kind of din you usually get when a team have won something.

Not that it helped the atmosphere in the dressing room. All the players were shattered when the realization of relegation had sunk in. When a club has been in the First Division for 27 years it is accepted as a right, and I think most of the lads that afternoon had the nasty feeling we had let down previous Spurs teams – especially the famous 'double' side.

The backing of the supporters, who had treated the occasion more like a wedding than a funeral, was some consolation. I'm sure the manner in which the fans stayed loyal was an inspiration which helped

Spurs gain promotion at the first attempt the following season. By then, of course, I had gone.

I didn't have long to wait for the first indication that I might have played my last game for Spurs.

Stories had started to appear in the newspapers that Keith was facing a goalkeeper problem; that Barry Daines was tired of being a reserve at the age of 26, and would ask to go rather than continue as my understudy. I never discussed the matter with Barry, but it was only natural if he was feeling in that kind of mood. Maybe that convinced Keith he would have to make a choice between us.

After the Leicester swan song, and before I joined Northern Ireland for the home international series, Spurs went on a short tour and it was on the return journey that I asked Keith, 'What's going to happen about the goalkeeper position next season?' I suppose my question was prompted by the rumours and, deep down, it could be that I felt in need of reassurance. If that was so, I didn't get it. I got a shock instead.

Keith's reply came out of the blue, and I recall it most vividly: 'Why, do you want to go?' I knew it was the beginning of the end. If you want to keep a player, the last thing you ask him is whether he wants to leave. I didn't need it spelled out.

In the next breath Keith added that he'd had an inquiry about me from Ipswich Town manager Bobby Robson a couple of months earlier in March, but at that time he felt he could not allow me to leave with the side battling against relegation. 'It would have been more than my job was worth to let you go then,' he said. Obviously, if I had left before Spurs went down, Keith could have been blamed. But he had clearly thought about it.

Later I was told Spurs had talked about a fee of £80,000, although Keith insisted he and Robson hadn't discussed a price. I believe him, for I can't imagine Spurs could have demanded that kind of fee for a player who had cost them only a third of that amount 13 years earlier. I felt I was worth it, but I didn't feel they had the right to ask it.

I thought of all the other players who had joined Spurs at much greater sums, had not put in anywhere near as much time with the club or played in half as many games and yet been awarded free transfers. If Spurs suddenly thought I couldn't do a job for them, I didn't think it was too much to expect them to say 'thanks for all you've done in the past' and let me go. That's the way I felt it should have been.

When I returned from the home internationals, and a World Cup tie for Northern Ireland in Iceland, the story of the Ipswich interest was in the papers. And again there was a mention of £80,000 being the value.

I telephoned Keith and challenged him on the price. 'Why, how much do you think you are worth?' was his come-back. 'I know what I'm worth, considering what is being paid for other goalkeepers,' I answered, 'but I don't think Spurs are entitled to a big fee after all my service, particularly as you seem to be giving me the elbow.' Keith knew my feelings, and I was aware that my days at Tottenham were numbered, but nothing more happened before I reported for pre-season training in mid-July.

Still, I wasn't keen to go – although I was flattered by the interest of Ipswich, one of the top clubs in the country. During that summer I was a bit dejected that Spurs were so willing to allow me to leave. I didn't doubt Keith's logical approach, on the basis that he was placing his bets on a younger man, but I had the sneaking feeling that one of the reasons the directors were in favour was that I probably was earning twice as much as Daines. I was reputed to be the biggest wage-earner at White Hart Lane, having been paid a basic £15,000 in that last season.

It wasn't bad money, yet it certainly wasn't an exceptional wage for a First Division star. And I'd only got that in that one season – ironically, when Spurs went down and I played just over half the games. Before that I was on £11,500.

Spurs had never been regarded among the top payers, and only a few years before I left I was getting £4,000 a year along with most of the other first-team players. We only got a rise when eight of us refused new contracts one summer and staged a mini-revolt. Then the money was almost doubled.

It is amazing when you contrast that with the present Spurs set-up, and Keith Burkinshaw must deserve a lot of the praise for the change which has taken place. A year after I left he went to Argentina to sign Ossie Ardiles and Ricky Villa and that must have transformed the wage structure.

The £15,000 I got in my last season with them was put into per-spective when I signed for Arsenal with a four-year contract at £20,000 a year. I was 32 and represented a gamble to Arsenal, yet they were willing to give me a long contract and pay £5,000 more than the club I'd served so long.

Admittedly, I got a nice pay day of around £25,000 after deductions from my overdue testimonial game at White Hart Lane. But for that

I had to thank the fans for turning out in support even though the team was going through a sticky spell. It didn't cost Spurs a penny, for I paid all the expenses on the night. In fact, all I got from the club was a lot of hassle because – after the fuss following Terry Neill's move to Highbury – the directors didn't want Arsenal to provide the opposition for that game. They suggested I play some other team, any team.

I remembered how Philip Beal had lost money on his testimonial game despite getting a crowd of nearly 20,000, when he had to pay a crippling fee to German club Bayern-Munich, so I asked if Spurs were ready to provide the cash guarantee required by a Continental or even top Scottish club. I was told that was quite out of the question – so I went ahead with the plan to play Arsenal and a crowd of over 28,000 showed they agreed with that decision.

All these thoughts were still going through my mind when I reported back for pre-season training, wondering what the future had in store. But things were normal at Cheshunt. We prepared in the usual fashion and I took part in the customary photo-call when all the photographers from the national papers come along for up-to-date shots of the professional staff.

Nothing was said or done to suggest my position was any different from any other year. I trained hard, spoke to Keith every day and the matter of a transfer wasn't mentioned once. I began to assume I would carry on where I had left off in May and I started thinking about some of the teams in the Second Division I'd never played against, and grounds where I had not appeared in the past.

I took part in a couple of friendly warm-up games, prior to the first-team squad's short pre-season tour of Sweden. I told my wife Eleanor I would be going as a matter of course, not thinking for a moment that I wouldn't.

A couple of days before the squad was due to leave, Keith called me to one side at Cheshunt. I was quite unprepared for what he said: 'Now that we've decided to let you go, the sooner you go the better. I don't want to take you to Sweden because you'll only be an embarrassment to Barry Daines.'

While I was letting the words sink in, Keith told me Bobby Robson would be ringing me at home at 5.30 that evening from Holland where Ipswich were on tour. He mentioned that Terry Neill had also been in touch with him and would be phoning after Robson. 'But I don't think you will have any sort of doubts which club to join,' he said, suggesting that Ipswich would be the obvious choice.

I was rocked on my heels, but I made it clear that I was capable of making up my own mind. And while I wasn't too bothered about a trip to Sweden, having been three-quarters of the way around the world a couple of times, I was in no mood to be either brainwashed or rushed into any decision.

Keith said he would be ringing me after I'd spoken to Robson and Neill to find out where I was going, because he wanted it all settled before he went to Sweden. I was blazing mad at the idea that, after more than 13 years with Spurs, I was being told to pick my next club in a few hours. 'I'll let you know in a week or so when you get back,' was my answer.

Now that my time was up at Tottenham, I went home to listen to what the managers of Ipswich and Arsenal had to offer and weighed up the advantages and disadvantages, while leaving them to ponder on what I expected.

On the morning Spurs were leaving for Sweden I felt I had to go down to White Hart Lane to say goodbye to all the players – some, like John Pratt and Steve Perryman, had been regular team-mates for a number of years – and to wish Barry Daines all the best. While I was in the car park, the directors all trooped out to join the coach and they walked past me without a single word of greeting. I never even got a 'good morning' from one of them. It was as though I didn't exist.

I've learned not to be surprised by anything in football, and I wouldn't say I'm a particularly emotional type. But if somebody had stuck a knife in me at that moment, it couldn't have hurt me more.

I can only think they had been told I was being awkward. If so they were misinformed. Or it could have been that the directors sensed I would be moving to Arsenal and weren't too pleased at the prospect.

One of the directors later told friends of mine that I had been greedy and asked for too much money to stay with Spurs. Since I had not requested a move, either verbally or in writing, and had not discussed cash with the manager or the Board, I was astonished at the statement. But if the directors were talking like that it was hardly surprising that the same impression was conveyed to the fans.

When I was eventually transferred to Arsenal there was no good-luck message from the Spurs directors. Their attitude seemed to be 'good riddance'. I had heard other former Spurs players say the same after they had left the club, and I guess there was no reason why I should have anticipated any different treatment. Yet it seemed such a sad and unnecessary way to end such a long association with one of soccer's most famous clubs.

I couldn't avoid comparing how the Spurs directors had acted with the gesture of Arsenal chairman, the late Denis Hill-Wood, following my testimonial game a few months earlier. On the morning after the match when I turned up at White Hart Lane I was handed an envelope from Mr Hill-Wood. It contained a fiver towards my testimonial fund to pay for his seat.

It was a smashing touch from a man I didn't know at that time. I remember thinking it was a bit of style, and subconsciously it may well have influenced the decision I was about to make in August 1977. Where next?

5

JOINING THE 'LONDON IRISH'

When I signed for Arsenal I didn't receive a signing-on fee of any kind, and I didn't come away from Highbury with a briefcase stuffed with banknotes. What I did get was an excellent contract which added up to £80,000 over four years, and a boost to my ego because of the length of the contract which would take me up to my 36th birthday. In the end the choice of Arsenal was an easy one, but I was flattered that three other top clubs – Aston Villa, Ipswich Town and Manchester United – all showed an interest in me.

Manchester United never got round to making a bid, because one of those quirks of fate which seem to crop up continually in football intervened. Manager Tommy Docherty was sacked. The Doc was looking for a goalkeeper, and his assistant Tommy Cavanagh was at that time coach to the Northern Ireland team. When he knew Spurs might let me go, Cav asked me if I fancied a move to Old Trafford. There could only be one answer to that – definitely. It seems the pair of them compiled a short list of two. Peter Shilton, then with Stoke City, was the other one. Then came the sacking of Docherty and the idea went up in smoke. Shilton joined Nottingham Forest about a month after my move to Arsenal and, luckily, things worked out fine for both of us.

Aston Villa were ready to pay the £45,000 Spurs wanted, but they didn't make their bid until I was about to sign on the dotted line at Highbury. Villa were playing in a pre-season tournament in Spain and took two goalkeepers on the trip, John Burridge and Jake Findlay. But things didn't go too well and manager Ron Saunders decided to look for a new goalkeeper. As things worked out, when Villa learned I was joining Arsenal they promptly snapped up Jimmy Rimmer – the man I was replacing. I'm sure Villa have never had any regrets, for Jimmy has been a model of consistency at Villa Park and in 1980–81 helped the club capture the League championship for the first time in 71 years.

Faced with a three-way choice, I would have gone to Arsenal rather than United or Villa. But I would be less than honest if I didn't admit that financial considerations could have taken me to Ipswich if they had come up with the money.

When Bobby Robson made the telephone call, as arranged with Keith Burkinshaw, his first question was, 'What sort of money do you want?' I replied '£30,000' and Bobby said 'What's that, in cash?' I can still hear myself saying 'Well, yes' and hoping he wouldn't hang up. In fact, what I had intended was £30,000 as a signing-on payment spread over a contract. But since he had suggested cash my reflexes took over and I quickly agreed.

Bobby pointed out that he would have to discuss the matter with his directors, and that he would phone me again when Ipswich returned from Holland. Since he had been keen enough to call me from there, a matter of hours before a pre-season game, I was hopeful he might at least come back with £20,000.

On reflection, I didn't feel such a sum was out of order, since I was convinced I could do a good job for Ipswich. Furthermore, the price had been cut to £45,000 from the £80,000 that was being mentioned two or three months earlier and, as Spurs were getting their pound of flesh, I felt I was entitled to mine.

We didn't get around to discussing the wages, but at that point I would have willingly settled for the same £15,000 a year I had received in that last season at Tottenham. So the total involved for Ipswich would hardly have been staggering.

Bobby did emphasize that he only wanted me for a couple of seasons because he had a high opinion of his own goalkeeper, Paul Cooper. His idea was that I could help Ipswich stabilize and pick up a trophy or two while Cooper developed. It was a reasonable enough plan which seemed to be of mutual benefit. Ipswich were also prepared to allow me to continue living in my Hertfordshire home and travel to Portman Road for training two or three days a week. Whether that would have been such a good idea, I'm not quite sure. That's all right when results are going well, but when things go wrong a manager tends to want you to turn up every day. But I have always been a player who trains hard and knew I would maintain a high level of fitness, so there wasn't any reason why the arrangement should not have worked for a couple of seasons.

Fate took a hand again, for in the following morning's papers, alongside the story that Ipswich were favourites to sign me, was the news that one of their strikers had been injured in the match in Holland and would probably miss the League kick-off. It caused

Bobby Robson to revise his priorities – it seemed he would require any available cash to strengthen his attack.

The £45,000 fee for me wasn't a big outlay, but when Ipswich did their sums they found that it would cost them £100,000 to give me a signing-on payment of around £20,000 after tax. The next thing I heard was that Bobby Robson had pulled out of the deal. Funny to think that, originally, I had expected to pay the tax when I quoted £30,000.

Secrets in soccer are non-existent, and the story that I priced myself out of that move has been going the rounds ever since.

I have often wondered whether Bobby Robson would have let me go after just a couple of seasons if I had signed for Ipswich. I acknowledge that at my age it must have seemed a gamble to him, but seeing how things went for me at Arsenal I would have represented a good buy over a longer period. But I've no complaints. It left the path open to move to Highbury and prevented any domestic upheaval. My children were able to stay at the same schools and I only had to drive an extra 15 minutes to either the training pitch or the ground.

I had kept Terry Neill informed and told him that if I got the cash I would go to Ipswich. He was equally straight and made it clear that there wouldn't be any signing-on fee from Arsenal, but promised me a good contract. He kept that promise, for the £20,000 a year was nearly twice what Spurs had been paying me two seasons earlier. Even then Terry went out on a limb in more than one respect. He already had a capable keeper in Rimmer who was younger, and I believe he went against the arguments of other people at Highbury in giving me a four-year contract. I'm glad I was able to justify his faith in me.

On the day the transfer was finalized, I was accompanied to Highbury by Peter Day – now Spurs' secretary – who was looking after Tottenham's interests. When we arrived he astounded me by asking if I was still sure I wanted to leave White Hart Lane.

I was unaware that he didn't know all the circumstances and pointed out that I had no option since it was Spurs' decision. Peter clearly didn't believe me, and told me to wait a few minutes while he telephoned Sweden. Whether he talked to the chairman or the manager I have no idea, but he came back with his tail between his legs and told me: 'Sorry Pat, you can go ahead and sign.'

Once I had put pen to paper I felt a great sense of relief. But I knew it would be like starting again. It was a challenge because I was determined to show Spurs they had made a big mistake, and I knew I must prove myself all over again with Arsenal. I couldn't exist on my reputation. I was also aware that some Arsenal fans would wonder if they were getting a Spurs throw-out. The readiness of Spurs to let me go would mean a lot of questions being asked.

It isn't the easiest of moves. Relations between the two North London clubs have always been distant, to put it in diplomatic terms, and since the end of the war only five players had 'crossed over'. The late Freddie Cox, an old-fashioned winger, went from Spurs to Arsenal in the late forties and played in two FA Cup finals – a record I was happy to beat with three Wembley appearances in my first three seasons at Highbury. Laurie Brown, who alternated between centre-half and centre-forward, moved in the opposite direction in the sixties and was a club-mate of mine at White Hart Lane. Then there was an exchange of wingers with Scottish international Jimmy Robertson going to Arsenal and David Jenkins to Spurs. And, of course, Willie Young made the same switch from White Hart Lane to Highbury a few months before me. Willie was given a rough time by the Arsenal fans in his first few games, but later became a great favourite of the crowd before moving on to Nottingham Forest.

It was obviously going to be more of a strain for me at Arsenal than if I had gone to Ipswich, where they regard Spurs as just another club. It didn't matter what I had done down the road for 13 years, it was how I shaped in my first few games at Arsenal that would be all important.

The tremendous rivalry between the fans is only matched at places like Liverpool and Manchester. Feelings were much fiercer on the terraces than in the respective dressing rooms – but, to be fair, that is only to be expected. Most supporters live in the same area all their lives, while players come and go. Usually they haven't grown up in the middle of Arsenal–Spurs arguments.

I had no real worries about how I would be received by the Arsenal crowd. They had always given me an even break when I was playing for Spurs, and, indeed, on one occasion gave me a fantastic reception. That was in April 1973, when Spurs went to Highbury a couple of days after I had been voted Footballer of the Year. When I ran out that afternoon it was to applause all round the ground and I had quite a lump in my throat.

My first game for Arsenal was at, of all places, Ipswich and we lost 1–0. It was the following Tuesday when I made my home début against Everton, and the North Bank took to me straight away. I got a special cheer of welcome, and those same fans have given me non-stop encouragement in the years which have followed. Even my mistakes have been excused.

I couldn't have made a better start at Highbury. We beat Everton 1–0 with a goal from Richie Powling, a talented youngster who suffered the cruel misfortune of having his career ruined by injury. It's the other side of the soccer coin: for every Kevin Keegan there is a Richie Powling.

Things continued to go well for me, and in my first six home games I conceded only one goal – and then we beat Leicester 2–1. It was certainly a happier beginning than I experienced with Spurs, for it wasn't all sunshine in my early days at White Hart Lane, when I was in and out of the side for two seasons before I clicked with the fans.

Footballers know in their heart of hearts that all supporters have the same attitude. If you are doing your stuff they back you all the way. If not . . . Where I have been lucky is that I have played for two clubs where the fans are particularly warm-hearted when things are going well, and I have enjoyed a fair degree of success at both Highbury and White Hart Lane.

Getting off on the right foot with Arsenal was clearly important for me and, here again, I could count myself fortunate that three of the back four were old friends and team-mates. In addition to Willie Young, the full-backs were Pat Rice and Sammy Nelson, both of whom had played in front of me for Northern Ireland in so many internationals. I knew what to expect from Pat and Sammy and it was a bonus that they understood my accent. And I knew Willie was a wholehearted big fellow who gave a hundred per cent in every game. In the four seasons we were together with Arsenal we developed a better understanding than we had had at Tottenham. He is certainly a far better player than most people realize.

The fourth member of the Arsenal defence was David O'Leary, who had been a first-team regular since he was 17. He didn't take long to impress me with his ability. David is a natural, the finest centre-half in Britain, and I know that former England manager Ron Greenwood always regarded it as a personal loss that he plays for the Republic of Ireland when he was born in London. Years ago that would automatically have qualified O'Leary for England, but FIFA changed the rules. Still, I can't imagine David in anything but an Irish shirt. He went to Dublin with his parents while still a baby, and is a typical Irish lad right down to his accent. He gets a tremendous kick whenever he represents his country, and I'll be surprised if he doesn't collect a record number of caps.

One of the reasons I was happy to join Arsenal was that, for as long as I'd known him, Sammy Nelson had always been singing the praises of the club. I don't think I've ever met another footballer who was such an out-and-out fan of the club he represented. Sammy was Arsenal through and through, as dedicated to Arsenal as any North Bank supporter.

Sammy spent 15 years at Highbury, arriving from Belfast in his early teens and leaving to join Brighton early in 1981–82 when he accepted he had little hope of regaining the left-back position from Kenny Sansom. He made more than 300 first-team appearances, always giving everything for the full 90 minutes – regardless of whether it was in the First Division or the Football Combination. It was a pity that, unlike his pal Pat Rice, he wasn't a regular member of the side which did the double in 1970–71. At that time he was understudy to another England left-back, Bob McNab.

Sammy's commitment to Arsenal landed him in trouble on the field on more than one occasion; sometimes he tended to act first and think afterwards and that brought him a quota of bookings and a suspension from time to time. Yet Sammy was always motivated by his dedication to Arsenal. When the team won he was on top of the world; defeat left him down in the dumps.

In my first three seasons at Highbury the club was dubbed the 'London Irish' by the cynics. Liam Brady and Frank Stapleton brought the number of regular Irishmen in the side to six. Once or twice it became seven when John Devine also came into the line-up. With Terry Neill as manager it may have looked like more than just coincidence to an outsider, and there were always a few cracks flying around the dressing room from the other lads. But I was never aware of the slightest resentment and the club enjoyed a run of success, finishing fifth, seventh and fourth in the First Division and creating a record with three consecutive FA Cup final appearances.

I had been aware of Arsenal's potential when I signed, and felt that at Highbury I might well realize my burning ambition of collecting a League championship medal.

At the end of that three-year spell, I honestly believed that Arsenal had a team good enough to go on and win the First Division. Graham Rix, who in my view has all that is needed to develop into a world-class player, was emerging in mid-field to dovetail with Brady. Alan Sunderland was forming a partnership with Stapleton which was loaded with goals.

The general view was that Arsenal were in need of just one more star player to push us right to the top. I think that even without another recruit the team would have been good enough, given freedom from serious injuries. But instead of being strengthened, Arsenal were weakened in the summer of 1980 – after a season in which we had reached the final of both the FA Cup and the European Cup-winners' Cup – when Brady left for Italy and Juventus. Then a year later we lost Stapleton to Manchester United. It was the kind of double blow which would have flattened any club.

When I joined Arsenal I didn't really know Liam or Frank. I had played against them and met them socially, but it went no deeper. I knew they were both excellent players, yet it was only when I was in the same side as them each week that I came to realize their true worth. I saw them both improve in front of my eyes as they got physically stronger, for don't forget Liam and Frank were still relative youngsters in their early twenties. I had the same feeling watching them as I did with David O'Leary: here were three players of incredible ability. In my quiet moments I used to keep my fingers crossed that I would stay in the Arsenal team long enough to see all three at their peak.

It didn't occur to me that I would remain at Highbury after Liam and Frank had left, and I have still never fully come to terms with the fact that it was unavoidable for them to go. It seems unbelievable that Arsenal should have received considerably less than a million and a half pounds in transfer fees for the pair of them, for they were worth at least three times as much. In fact, they were priceless as far as Arsenal were concerned.

Both moves were the direct outcome of the introduction of freedom of contract, which gives every player the right to change clubs – for a transfer fee either mutually agreed or settled by an independent tribunal – if he so desires. I don't blame Liam or Frank for exercising that right.

When speculation was increasing in 1979–80 that Liam would be leaving at the end of that season, I kept hoping that Arsenal would find a way of holding on to him. I was deflated when the news finally broke that Liam had gone, and then went through all the same emotions a year later when Frank moved as well.

We had the makings of a great team, and it is sad that even a club as big as Arsenal felt they were unable to keep it intact. One of the most famous clubs in the world lost out to first Juventus and then Manchester United for purely financial reasons, for I am convinced that Liam and Frank would have remained had Arsenal come up with the money.

I have frequently been asked how I would have felt knowing that another Arsenal player was getting double or treble my wages. My answer is that every player has to get the best possible deal for himself. When he eventually signs a new contract he is presumably happy with the terms, so there is an obligation to abide by it whether it's for a year, two years or even three years, regardless of what any team-mate is being paid. It's no good looking over your shoulder and feeling resentful.

I know there is inevitably talk of a wage structure within a club, but I don't think that applies at Arsenal or at any other First Division club. Right through the 22 teams there are some players getting twice or three times as much as others.

Only in the five or ten years which followed the abolition of the maximum wage, back in the early sixties, did clubs try to keep the differential between regular first-team members as narrow as possible. It was claimed, and I imagine a lot of people would agree, that such a policy was essential because soccer is a team game. But whether the pure-minded like it or not, the fact remains there are star players whose bargaining power is far greater than that of most of their team-mates.

The same yardstick has to be applied to players who fill the same positions with different clubs. I have been gratified when I've been called one of the world's top goalkeepers and regarded as at least the equal of Peter Shilton. But while I was reading, or hearing, that kind of praise, I knew that Shilton was earning twice the money I was getting at Arsenal.

I'm sure that the other Arsenal players would have accepted the situation whatever Brady and Stapleton had been paid to stay, but clearly the directors felt they had to apply some kind of limit. It's hard to strike a balance when you know the next player to reach the end of a contract would base his demands on what Liam and Frank had received. That's the other side of the story.

Yet Liam and Frank had been at Highbury from the age of 15 or 16, and had given wonderful service and proved their loyalty. So any payment could be regarded as a reward for the past as much as an investment for the future. Both were impossible to replace.

The alternative was to lash out a big fee to get somebody to try and fill the gaps; and while transfer prices may be lower on the Continent because of the various systems governing the movement of players, a foreigner would expect a massive signing-on fee. So it's a moot point who deserves to cash in.

Obviously a lot of sheer stubbornness, call it 'principle' if you like, came into the negotiations between Arsenal and the two players. Because neither had originally cost the club a penny in transfer outlay, they both probably felt they had not been particularly well paid for much of their time at Highbury and that they would never be in a stronger position to get the club to cough up.

It was a kind of love–hate relationship which grew and grew, with perhaps both parties cutting off their noses to spite their faces to a certain extent. But, in the final analysis, Liam and Frank would have stayed if the money had been put on the table.

A lot has been written that Brady was more interested in the challenge of sampling soccer and life abroad. I don't believe that and I think my view will be endorsed when Liam's contract in Italy expires, despite the tremendous success he enjoyed with Juventus, collecting two championship medals, and a taste of the European Cup.

There's no way Stapleton wanted to uproot himself from London and move to Manchester, and burden himself with a transfer tag of nearly a million pounds. He was in much the same position as I had been at Tottenham, with a reputation which could survive a few poor games, and regarded as a great favourite by the crowd. With United he had to go out and do it all over again. The fact that he married a Manchester girl in the summer of 1981 may have influenced his final choice of club, but his negotiations with Arsenal started long before.

Frank said he had no plans to leave if Arsenal came up with the money. But he had shaken hands with United manager Ron Atkinson when he received an improved offer from Arsenal which was almost as good, and at that stage felt he couldn't go back on his word.

I accept it was a matter of principle which held Arsenal back rather than counting the cost, for constant trips to the Continent by manager Terry Neill, coach Don Howe and the scouting staff in the search for a replacement – not to mention the time involved – proved expensive. And they still couldn't find another Stapleton.

Arsenal's financial loss may well have been considerably greater. It can never be proved, but if Frank had been getting goals at his usual rate the team might have made a much better start to 1981–82. If we had been scoring regularly at home, and winning with a bit of style, attendances at Highbury could have been nearer 40,000 than 20,000. Arsenal might also have made a bigger impact in cup football instead of making early exits from the UEFA Cup, League Cup and FA Cup, so how can you assess the eventual bill for Stapleton's departure?

Even the other Arsenal players probably lost out, on bonus money, for everybody in the team shares from the success of the stars. There's a spin-off right the way through, from the manager downwards, which benefits the rest of the staff. That's another reason why there would have been very little resentment in the dressing room if Liam and Frank had remained.

You can liken the situation to strikers who score regularly, even if not working as hard on the field as the rest of the side. While they are popping the ball in the net, nobody minds too much. When the goals stop, they are accused of being lazy. It's human nature, and you'll never get a perfect balance.

The big wages now paid in the First Division to the top men, and the gap it creates, admittedly breeds a touch more jealousy than in my days at White Hart Lane when the whole Spurs team was underpaid in my opinion. But it's still marginal.

If you are only getting £80, each, a week you know everybody is in the same boat. Yet the players who are doing their stuff regularly think it's unfair they are paid no better than others who are not pulling their weight.

I can only speak for myself, but I wish Brady and Stapleton had got the money they were asking from Arsenal. It might have been exceptional – but then they are both exceptional footballers. And, anyway, it would be nice to know a couple of millionaires.

6

THE IDEAL PARTNERSHIP

A football club can only have one manager, but it takes two men at the top to run it successfully these days and Arsenal have an ideal partnership in Terry Neill and Don Howe. I'm tempted to say that Terry and Don go together like Morecambe and Wise, and risk the obvious crack that I'm labelling them as a couple of comedians. But as a soccer double act they dovetail perfectly. Both are suited to the roles they fill at Highbury.

You just can't have a manager running the whole show, for it would often place him in an impossible position. Imagine trying to haggle over a contract with a player behind a desk, and then putting on a track-suit and attempting to get the best out of him in training or in a match. How can you tell a star footballer he is the greatest thing on two legs, in a bid to gee him up for a game, when you've already insisted he isn't worth the wages he is asking?

Terry and Don divide those responsibilities, yet are always around to support each other when necessary. They complement each other, but if I had to put them into separate pigeon holes I'd say that Terry usually relies upon a softly, softly approach while Don is the hard man of the duo.

I've known Terry a lot longer. I played with him many times for Northern Ireland, where he was first captain and then player-manager. He took over as manager of Spurs for two seasons and then, of course, signed me for Arsenal. I have always found him easy to get on with – though, inevitably, we've had our differences. He's got an easy-going nature, but can be tough when the need arises, and his record as both a player and a manager speaks for itself. He has achieved a lot of success on and off the field.

When I first met him, as a team-mate in the Irish side, Terry was in his early twenties, but even at that age it was a fair bet he would eventually become a manager when his playing days ended. He would always say his piece about tactics at team meetings while others like myself preferred to sit and listen. He is a good talker and although he is sometimes inclined to a touch of blarney, Terry has very definite ideas about the game and what he wants from players.

We developed a good understanding when we played together for Northern Ireland. He was an automatic choice at centre-half for many years, and held the record for most Irish caps until he retired and I eventually took it from him.

I liked playing with Terry. He had two good feet, was good in the air and possessed bags of confidence. He had an excellent build for a centre-half, never having any weight problems, and always gave a hundred per cent throughout the 90 minutes. Most of all he was reliable: you always knew what he was going to do, and that is a re-assuring feeling for any goalkeeper.

When he took over at Tottenham he had a task which was doubly difficult. Not only was Terry succeeding Bill Nicholson – who was so highly respected by the Spurs players who felt more than a little upset Bill had been allowed to leave – but the team had also made a disastrous start to the 1974–75 season.

We had lost five of our opening six League games, against Manchester City (twice), Ipswich, Liverpool and even newly-promoted Carlisle. The only good result was a 2–0 home victory over Derby. In addition to being at the very foot of the First Division, we got a terrible 4–0 League Cup hammering from Middlesbrough on the night before Terry arrived. What made it worse was that game was played at White Hart Lane, so morale among the fans was as low as it was in the dressing room.

It often happens that a new manager sparks off a temporary revival by a club, and Spurs duly won the first two games under Terry by following up a 2–1 home victory over West Ham by a 3–2 success away to Wolves. But it was a brief respite, for the next three matches ended in defeat and nobody was under any illusions. We clearly faced a season-long struggle to avoid relegation, and only escaped by beating Leeds in the very last game.

Although I knew him well, Terry kept our relationship on the right level as manager and player. He didn't ask for my opinion about the strengths and weaknesses of the Spurs players, preferring to make his own judgment.

I was grateful not to be put on the spot in that respect, but Terry did have a habit of embarrassing me by indirect praise after a defeat. He would come into the dressing room and tell the rest of the team, 'You'll ruin Pat's confidence if you keep making silly mistakes' or, 'You'll break the goalkeeper's heart if you carry on like this'. I know it was intended as a compliment to me, but I'd have been happier if he hadn't said it. It made it look as if I was a favourite, and in a football club that can be as uncomfortable as being teacher's pet at school. I got a fair amount of ribbing from the other players, but it was all good natured.

Terry deserves a lot of credit for saving Spurs from the drop into the Second Division that season, mainly because he refused to panic when results were bad and never showed any sign of personal pressure. That is vital in such a situation, for when a manager is clearly worried it doesn't take very long for pessimism to spread right through a club.

This outward appearance of calm is undoubtedly one of Terry's assets. It obviously served him well in his first season at Highbury when Arsenal had a lean time, and again early in 1981–82 when – after the loss of Frank Stapleton – he came in for some scathing criticism for not strengthening the team.

There was a mistaken impression at the time that he was indifferent to the departure of Stapleton, but nothing could have been further from the truth so far as both Terry and Don were concerned. They knew better than anybody else the extent of the loss of Frank and Liam Brady before him – because they depend upon players of that calibre to make them better managers and coaches. It affects their livelihood.

Terry kept being quoted in the press at that time that he had faith in the players at Highbury, but that doesn't mean he was sitting on his backside doing nothing. He put in a lot of hours assessing possible replacements. Apart from the clamour from the fans, he and Don were only too aware that the other Arsenal players were waiting for new signings to boost the team.

Terry's hardest season was probably his first as Arsenal manager, before the appointment of Don Howe as his right-hand man. I was still at Tottenham at that time, but I was told later by some of the Arsenal lads that things were pretty bleak after they were knocked out of the FA Cup by 4–1 in a fifth-round tie at Middlesbrough. One of Terry's problems upon returning to Highbury as boss was the presence of a number of former team-mates who were still players with the club. Some had been there longer than him, and understandably found it strange – if not downright difficult – to accept Terry's new role.

Footballers are just as cynical as workers in other walks of life, and it is hard for a manager to command respect from players who were once his equals and often his companions on a night out after an away game or on an end-of-season tour. Terry was away from Highbury for six years, at Hull and Tottenham, and had to come to terms with the situation upon his return. Bill Nicholson at Tottenham and Don Revie at Leeds perhaps represent the two outstanding examples of men who bridged the gap successfully, and it might have been slightly easier for them because both were rather dour, single-minded types.

It may seem an odd thing to say, but players generally regard their relationships with manager and coach as 'Us and Them'. You naturally see everything from your own side of the fence and don't have too much sympathy for those on the other side. Your chief concern is always your own form. A great deal of rubbish is spouted that players do a superb job for the team. The principal concern is to do well yourself, and that includes having a clear conscience about giving maximum effort and maintaining peak physical condition. Then everybody reaps the benefit – player, team and club. That is the only way for any footballer to be a good 'team man'.

In any assessment of Terry Neill it has to be said that he has not changed since the first day I met him. His smooth-talking style, which may not be everybody's cup of tea, is not something he has acquired as manager of Spurs and Arsenal. It has always been part of his make-up.

Terry doesn't always do things strictly by the book. He is willing to try a gimmick if it brings results and benefits the team, a classic example of this happening at the end of his first season as manager of Spurs when we had to beat Leeds in that final match at White Hart Lane to stay in the First Division.

The game was played on a Monday night and we spent the weekend, after losing to Arsenal at Highbury on the Saturday, at a North London hotel now favoured by England for pre-match build-ups. It was impossible not to think continually about just what was at stake and whether we were good enough to beat Leeds. A few of us had secret doubts.

Maybe the uncertainty was showing, for on the Sunday afternoon Terry produced his 'twelfth man' – a hypnotist. The idea was to put all the players under the influence so that they would rise to the occasion. It seemed an ironic tactic to use against Leeds of all clubs, for it was real Don Revie stuff.

I was one of only two players who said 'thanks, but no thanks' to a hypnotic session – I think John Pratt was the other. I felt that it wouldn't help me. If I was going to do my stuff, and enable Spurs to stay in the First Division, I was capable of doing it under my own power.

All the rest of the lads trooped in one at a time for the treatment, it was a bit like seeing people go to confession. When they were put under the spell they were urged to remember their best-ever game – one or two said later they had problems on that score – so that they would perform up to the same high standard the following night. I recall seeing Cyril Knowles so 'gone' that he was stretched across the top of two chairs, his head resting on one and his feet on the other, while he responded to instructions to take my weight. I sat on Cyril and he didn't flinch. It was impressive, just like something you might see on television.

Despite my scepticism, I must admit Terry's idea was a success because it gave us all a laugh, relaxed the lads and helped to pass the time. Whether it influenced the result I'll leave you to decide, but Spurs beat Leeds 4–2 and Cyril Knowles scored twice from left-back.

Arsenal haven't needed a hypnotist since I've been at Highbury – at times we've been accused by the cynics of putting our crowd to sleep – yet I'm sure Terry wouldn't hesitate to call upon one if he thought it would enable the club to win a vital game. But I doubt if Don Howe would approve, it's not his way of doing things.

The usual pre-match drill for a home match is that the first team report at South Herts Golf Club at 11.30 on a Saturday morning. We have a meal which starts with soup or corn flakes and is followed by poached or scrambled eggs. In my early days at Tottenham the menu was steaks and rice, but now it seems the dieticians have worked out that that kind of meal takes too long to digest before it becomes beneficial. Soup and eggs, we are told, are ideal three hours or so before kick-off.

After eating, some of the Arsenal lads play snooker, others settle down to watch the football programme on the television. Around one o'clock comes the tactical talk. Terry starts it off, usually by reminding us of the importance of the game, then Don takes over with a more detailed break-down.

Arsenal have the opposition watched in their previous match – the regular 'spy' is the former club captain and England full-back George Male – and Don pinpoints one or two of the opposing players with the emphasis on any recent signings. But his main theme is how Arsenal are going to play on that particular day.

Don is a top-class coach, and I always feel it is unfair when I read that his tactics are based on defence. I can honestly tell you he is not defensively minded – on the contrary, he would love to play with four forwards. But since Arsenal haven't got enough players of that type, he knows his job is to get the best out of those at his command . . . while still urging them to attack whenever possible. He likes his midfield men to get into the opposition's penalty area as often as they can, and his back players to move up in support when they can do so without taking unnecessary risks. But equally he demands that everybody works back if the other team are going forward, and that includes our strikers.

There's no doubt that Don is very demanding, and he tends to become angry and frustrated if players don't respond to his own code. I realize at times how events must have snowballed during the four years he was manager of West Bromwich Albion. He spent his hey-day as an England full-back at West Bromwich and when he returned to take charge in 1971, after helping Arsenal pull off the League championship and FA Cup double, he must have been full of hope and ambition. It didn't work out that way, and perhaps the reason was that Don tried to do too much himself and that his expectations were too great.

To some extent, I think Don lives in the past when it comes to what he can demand from players in terms of dedication – even compared to when I came into the game. Habits have changed, like it or not. He would like to recreate the discipline of his own playing days, when players wouldn't go out for a drink after Wednesday night. Nowadays players have come to expect far more freedom: whilst only a small minority abuse it, the majority would resent being told how to spend their spare time.

I remember that when I joined Spurs, with two internationals for Northern Ireland to my credit, I went into digs with Cyril Knowles, who was an England Under-23 full-back and had just cost £45,000 from Middlesbrough. We were both first-team players, but we knew better than to keep late hours. So our mid-week social life consisted of one or two visits to the cinema. We were always in by eleven o'clock. Our landlady, Mrs Galloway, had been looking after Spurs players for a number of years and there's no doubt she was instructed by the club to keep a motherly eye on them. She would have regarded it as part of her duty to report us if we had stayed out after 'curfew' regularly, and we were aware of the fact.

It couldn't happen today at First Division level. Those old-fashioned digs – Mrs Galloway got around £4 to £5 apiece from us – are a thing of the past. A player transferred from another club who is still single expects to go into a hotel or a flat of his own.

Don undoubtedly regrets the changing scene, because he feels discipline is essential in all aspects of soccer. When it was announced he was returning to Highbury in August 1977, a few days after I had signed, I recall some of the older players saying immediately that things would tighten up in terms of time-keeping and being on the ball generally. And they were delighted about it – they were sure it would benefit the club. After five years I can wholeheartedly testify they were right.

That's not to say I haven't had my disagreements with Don. He can be a hard taskmaster and more cutting with his remarks than Terry after a poor performance. All the lads feel it more deeply when Don has had a go at them. It can really hurt.

He's sorted me out several times. As far as he's concerned, reputations mean absolutely nothing. It doesn't matter how big a player may be, Don doesn't play favourites. Malcolm Macdonald, Alan Hudson and Liam Brady all suffered a typical Howe tongue lashing.

Once he really tore into Liam, so much so that I thought Don went way over the top with his criticism – and I told him so. It was one occasion when I disagreed with Don, and by no means the only time. But I learned you seldom win an argument with a coach in the end. They seem to have a built-in resistance to any backchat, as though regarding it as an excuse, and it's a very rare occasion when Don admits he may be wrong – and then it's only 'maybe'.

I don't have a lot to say in team talks, yet I've never been afraid to say my piece if I think I'm justified. That, in my view, is what being a member of a team is all about. I don't believe any manager or coach really wants to have 11 yes-men without an opinion between the lot of them.

Don, like all coaches, can pinpoint an error which led to a goal against Arsenal even if it means going back seven or eight moves to when the mistake was made. Understandably, he takes it badly if the mistake was the result of a player not carrying out pre-match instructions.

There are, of course, two ways of looking at every goal. Don expects our defenders to get the ball clear, whatever the opposition players are doing – then he expects our forwards to go up the other end and score, regardless of the efforts of opposing defenders.

Don likes his players to be aggressive because he feels that reflects their honesty, their willingness to give a hundred per cent. But he never encourages them to go beyond the rules, and I've never heard him tell our defenders to go out and kick people. He just wants them to tackle hard and win the ball. It was the way he played himself, for he was a stylish full-back and a clean tackler who was noted for his distribution once he had possession. Don made the most of his attributes, for he wasn't the quickest defender I've seen.

If he wants an opposing player put out of the game, he wants it done by close marking so that they are denied space and rendered as ineffective as possible. It's not easy against somebody like Kevin Keegan who never stops running, but Don insists it can be done if the marker sticks to his task and doesn't lose his concentration.

I like to analyse my own game from time to time, especially if I've had an afternoon where I know I've been at fault. I'm not talking about giving away a soft goal so much as a failure to catch the ball as cleanly as I might. Then I'm always prepared to listen carefully to any advice.

Don has had a go at every department of my game at some stage, my distribution, my kicking and my handling. He isn't always right. Sitting on the touchline, or in the stand, a coach doesn't always see everything which takes place in a crowded goalmouth. There are occasions when a team-mate can impede you and pose a bigger problem than an opposing striker.

A goalkeeper has to have a mind of his own. If he is constantly being told he should go for every cross from the wing and every through ball, he can end up going for things he hasn't a chance of getting and creating confusion in his own defence. There was a spell when Don was critical if I failed to reach every ball hit to the near post, or just short of it. Often, I knew I couldn't get through the ruck of players, friend and foe, in my path – but Don didn't accept my judgment. He wanted me to clamber over everybody in my way if necessary, and, frankly, that wasn't on.

We agreed to differ on that subject, but after watching the difficulties that other goalkeepers got into when trying things his way, I think Don eventually felt I had a case. I don't think he ever actually said so, and I certainly didn't say I told you so. I've got too much respect for the fellow and, anyway, so much of football is a matter of opinion.

I suppose most of my rows with Don have concerned overkicking. At times I don't think enough has been made of my ability to drop-kick a ball at least three-quarters of the length of the field. I know that at that distance I can drop a ball within ten yards of one of our strikers, who would have time to make up the ground. When Arsenal had front men like Malcolm Macdonald or Frank Stapleton it could be particularly useful. Both of them, and especially Malcolm, had the pace to burst clear and get in a shot at goal.

Don likes me to try that with my very first drop-kick in a game, in the hope of catching opposing defenders on the hop. But, after that, he prefers more variation, pointing out that if our own defenders and midfield men have dropped back, looking for a short throw, it is pointless to kick the ball 60 or 70 yards when there's nobody in support of the front players. I accept that argument, I just think I ought to try it more often.

As with any tactical ploy, much depends on the team you are playing and how they react to it. Some teams will let you have the ball in your own third of the pitch and just drop back, when you can play up through them as long as you like. Then you meet others who push up and refuse to allow you time and space to use the ball. That's when I get plenty of pass-backs.

Whereas Don, maybe recalling his own playing days when the ball was heavier and more difficult to control, doesn't feel that the long kick poses enough problems enough of the time, Northern Ireland's Billy Bingham loves me to knock balls up to the edge of the opposing 18-yard line so that our forwards and midfield players can move up quickly. It works well because we've got a couple of big fellows up front who can knock the ball down.

The Irish team isn't equipped for a slow build-up from the back so, certainly in Belfast with a big and enthusiastic crowd behind us, the manager believes my long kicking can help to put any visiting international side under pressure. This is particularly true against continentals who are geared to dealing with a slower, if more accurate, method of attack.

When big kicking becomes overkicking it's a waste of everybody's energy, including mine. When it works out it becomes the simplest ploy in football, with one forward nodding the ball on and another going through to score.

I hope I have not given a false impression either of my relationship with Don or my opinion of him as a coach. It could not be higher. But it would be wrong to suggest that at the top level there is never a cross word between a coach and player. It is all for the good of the team and, so far as Don and I are concerned, there is never any ill feeling once we've said our piece.

The only real bust-up we ever had had nothing to do with tactics. It concerned turning up late for training one morning, and the outcome was that I was fined for the only time in my Arsenal career. The fine was £100 – and I refused point-blank to pay it.

Alan Sunderland, Willie Young and I all lived near each other and used to take turns to drive to the training ground at London Colney. We always left around 9.15 to allow ample time to arrive before ten o'clock. One morning it was my day to act as chauffeur, and there was a crash in front of us on the road. It was impossible to move, for the cars involved had to be towed away and we were held up for 20 minutes and eventually turned up five or six minutes late.

Don was livid and there was an unbelievable scene. He refused to make any allowance for what had happened. He was living in Wolverhampton and driving down each morning, leaving his home by seven o'clock in order to give himself plenty of time to get to the ground. He couldn't accept there was any excuse for those of us travelling much shorter distances. Terry understood my position, but he didn't want to let Don down. He knew, as we all did, how strongly Don felt that club rules must be obeyed.

When secretary Ken Friar notified me I was to be fined £100, I made it clear I had no intention of paying. I thought it was unfair in the circumstances. It was a genuine matter of principle, and I was prepared to fight it all the way – even if it resulted in being put on the transfer list.

In the end we had a meeting about it, and Terry said they were going to scrap the fine on this occasion but that if it happened in the future any player reporting late would automatically have his money docked. Don promptly stood up and declared: 'That's it! Next time we make a rule which is broken and the fines aren't paid, I'm going to walk out of the place for good.'

That's the sort of bloke he is and I am sure he meant every word at the time. I think he has mellowed a bit since, but I wouldn't want to put it to the test and I'm sure the same goes for every other Arsenal player.

7

HOOLIGANISM

Bottles, coins, darts, door-knobs and stones – all have made direct hits on me over the years. Once I was even the target for a billiard ball. In fact, you name anything which could be used as a missile by hooligan fans and I've had it chucked at me.

Hooligans have been a soccer menace as long as I've been in the game, with their exploits both inside and outside grounds filling thousands of inches of newspaper space and being shown on television. The bad publicity has done tremendous harm to football and undoubtedly kept many decent folk away.

I'm glad, for financial reasons, that I wasn't a professional footballer in the days of the maximum wage. I've earned good money compared with players of the forties, fifties and even the early sixties, who got only peanuts for their efforts. Looking back on the vast crowds they attracted all of them were underpaid to a disgraceful extent. But I admit I envy my predecessors in one respect. They played when spectators were much better behaved, when there was more good humour among the rival fans and youngsters were proud – instead of scared – of turning up at an away match sporting the colours of the club they support.

Old-timers will recount stories of how, in a packed ground, young children were passed over the heads of the crowd to the front of the terraces so they could get a good view of the game. Old-timers? Well, I can remember seeing it happen myself when a young lad at international matches at Windsor Park, Belfast.

Now, sadly, those days have gone forever. It only takes a handful of lunatics to spark off trouble, and when it comes to throwing missiles then a goalkeeper is the obvious Aunt Sally because he is the nearest.

I remember being hit by a bottle on a February day in 1975 when playing for Spurs against Everton at Goodison Park. Whoever threw it was some marksman, for it must have travelled at least 15 to 20 yards before smacking me on the back of the head. And since it was a Coke bottle he must have been a teetotaller.

Play was at the other end, so I was standing in my usual position a few yards off my line and the bottle must have sailed right over the top of the goal. I wasn't knocked out, but I was dazed and I went down on one knee to draw the attention of the referee and the other players – they were all facing the other way and hadn't seen what had happened. I felt the back of my head, looking for blood, but fortunately it hadn't broken my skin.

When the referee summed up the situation, he called on the Spurs trainer and handed the bottle to a policeman behind the goal. I didn't make an official complaint, though naturally the referee later reported the incident to the FA and the Football League. I couldn't blame Everton, or condemn the rest of their fans, for the stupidity of one fellow in a crowd of 30,000.

Ironically, there was already an arc cut out of the terracing behind the goal at Goodison to try and prevent such a thing happening because another Spurs goalkeeper, Bill Brown, had been hit by a dart in a match a few years earlier. And the Everton officials, and players, were full of apologies after the game. But that's all I got, apart from a head-ache, that afternoon for Spurs finished 1–0 losers. There was no bonus to ease the pain.

One souvenir I still possess is a dart which was thrown at me when playing for Spurs at Carlisle. I was dead lucky on that occasion, for I actually felt the dart pass through my hair and saw it stick in the pitch in front of me. It could so easily have been sticking in the back of my head.

At first I couldn't believe my eyes. The thought that some idiot could risk doing me permanent harm seemed incredible at the time. After all, it didn't require any real courage on his part when sur-rounded by his mates – and though it must have been thrown from a fair distance it wasn't that difficult to hit somebody my size.

Carlisle United might have had their ground closed if that incident had come to light, but I didn't say a word. Well, to be strictly accurate, I did tell manager Bill Nicholson after the game, but Bill just shrugged it off. He's like me in that respect, he didn't want to make a fuss. One of the dangers when such an incident gets widely reported is that it might encourage some other nut-case to copy it at another ground the following week. I have often wondered what Bill's reaction would have been if that dart had not missed by only a fraction of an inch.

Later in my career, I was struck by a dart in an Arsenal match on the Nottingham Forest ground – and this time it stuck. It is all some-thing of a blur in my mind, but I had moved forward in anticipation of a back-pass when I felt something strike the inside of my arm. As play swung away, I looked down and for a moment I couldn't believe what I saw – it was a dart, and it was firmly embedded in my arm. I pulled it out and my arm started to go numb because it had stuck in a muscle. My first reaction was 'I hope this doesn't get any worse'. Luckily, although my arm was a bit stiff and sore, it did not restrict my movement for the rest of the game.

I tossed the dart into the back of the goal, and then I saw a Forest steward walking round – presumably to take it away. So I put it inside my cap and waited until the interval before producing it in the dressing room. Arsenal coach Don Howe, like the majority of the players on the field, had not seen the incident happen, but when I produced the dart he took it straight to the referee.

The incident had also gone unnoticed in the press box and there was plenty of publicity when the reporters at the City Ground learned about it after the game. They even had some evidence, because one photographer was pretty sharp that afternoon and took a photograph of the dart sticking in my left arm. He was able to scoop rival photographers as, like me, they were not expecting it.

As at Carlisle, my initial feeling was to keep it quiet – but there is another angle to consider in contrast to the risk of imitation. It's the possibility that if the culprit gets away with it once, he might repeat the act at the next game and strike some unsuspecting goalkeeper in the eye. That thought is enough to make your blood run cold, and makes you wonder if the dart-thrower really considered the possible consequences.

Nobody was more upset about that episode than Forest boss Brian Clough, who sent me an amusing letter of apology. I got another from the Nottingham Forest Supporters' Club asking me not to judge all their fans by the action of one maniac. I didn't, for I have always liked playing at the ground.

One of the reasons why I have no ill-will towards supporters of Everton, Carlisle and Forest is that I know missiles can be thrown at any ground. Once I even came under bombardment from West Ham fans when I was playing for Spurs – at White Hart Lane.

That afternoon I thought I was being hit by air-gun pellets because the barrage was so constant. Then I discovered it was steel staples being fired by elastic bands or catapults, and I gathered up a handful of them and handed them to a policeman. I've been the target of a pea-shooter attack in the past, but those steel staples were much more frightening because one of them could easily have blinded me.

Perhaps my worst experience came in a match with Manchester

United, who have always had more than a fair share of wild men following them around the country. Played at White Hart Lane, it had been a tremendous game and Spurs, after being 1–0 down, came back to take the lead with a couple of typical goals from Jimmy Greaves. After Jimmy's second, the United fans started tossing bottles on to the pitch at my end. Before I realized what had happened, United broke away in search of an equalizer and Bobby Charlton gained possession and came tearing towards me in full flight. It was only when I was advancing from my line that I spotted the broken bottles littering the goalmouth.

The scene is still vivid in my mind . . . I don't believe I shall ever forget it. I was wondering what to do, whether to throw myself down to challenge Bobby, and risk serious injury from the ugly lumps of glass, or stay on my feet and allow him a better scoring chance.

A lifetime seemed to be crowded into the space of a second, and I was the most relieved footballer in the business when a Spurs defender hurtled forward to tackle Charlton and whip the ball from him right on the edge of the area. I still can't tell you what I would have done.

I also got away unscathed when playing for Arsenal at Norwich when the fans showered handfuls of coins at me for the entire second half. The Norwich supporters who stand behind that particular goal must have had money to spare for they seemed to be throwing dozens of 10p pieces at a time.

The coins rattled against the iron fence a couple of yards behind me whenever Norwich got the ball near our penalty area or forced a corner. To say it was distracting is to put it mildly: I was trying to concentrate upon the play while half-expecting to get hit any second. It might sound funny, but a coin flicked at great speed can be highly dangerous, especially when it has been sharpened beforehand, as sometimes happens.

What was really crazy was that the Norwich fans had been guilty of exactly the same thing a few weeks earlier when Aston Villa goalkeeper Jimmy Rimmer had been hit. For the Arsenal game, the club stationed police among the crowd behind the offending goal. It didn't have the slightest effect – unless you have one policeman for every three or four fans they are powerless. If somebody goes to a game with the intention of throwing missiles, whatever the shape or size, it seems, sadly, that it's impossible to prevent it. Yet, especially at corner-kicks, the coins could just have easily have struck – and badly hurt – a Norwich player. It shows the kind of brainless people who do such things.

By comparison, the day I became a 'snowman' at Hillsborough, during a third round FA Cup-tie between Arsenal and Sheffield Wednesday, was kid's stuff. The score was level at 1–1 and each time Wednesday surged upfield in search of a winner I was pelted with snowballs. That was relatively harmless, but still very distracting. If you are hit on the head or the back of the neck by a snowball, the natural reaction is to turn round to find out what is coming your way. Dozens were hurled in my direction that afternoon and I had a most uncomfortable second half.

It seems at times that the poor goalkeeper has no chance, either on or off the field. Another hazard is when stones or other objects are thrown at the team coach leaving a ground after an away game. One of the worst incidents happened after Chelsea's FA Cup replay at Hull in January 1982 when a missile was thrown through the window of the coach on the way back to London – and, sure enough, it was the goalkeeper who was hit. Poor Steve Francis, only 17, had to have a bad cut stitched and he earned my admiration when he bounced back to play in another Cup-tie against Wrexham less than 48 hours later. Young Steve, in his first season, must have wondered if football was as glamorous as he had been led to believe when that kind of thing can happen long after a game has finished.

It is something I haven't suffered, though there was a near thing when Arsenal were driving away from Molyneux after a match with Wolves and a brick hit the window of our coach. It didn't shatter the glass, but the sound it made – and the thought of what might have been – scared the life out of the entire team.

Sometimes you can even be in trouble before the kick-off. When Spurs and Chelsea met at White Hart Lane towards the end of 1974–75, with both clubs in real danger of relegation, the start was delayed because hundreds of fans of both teams ran on to the pitch to get to grips with each other. They were still being hustled off by the police and officials when the referee got the go-ahead to send the players out in the hope that our appearance would help restore some kind of order.

As we walked on in single file through the milling fans I was deliberately kicked a couple of times. One fellow – and he certainly wasn't a skinhead – lashed out at me. I can only presume he was a Chelsea supporter who felt he might be able to help his team by his action. As it happened, he got quite a surprise when I belted him back. It's not my usual form, but it was one of those occasions when I had no intention of just taking it.

It's the only time I've ever struck a spectator but, like other players,

I have wondered what to do when a fan runs on to the pitch and comes towards you. You never quite know whether he is coming over to pat you on the back, or whether he is in the mood for trouble. Then you risk getting a punch or a kick which could cause injury and perhaps prevent you finishing the game.

If he does prove to be in aggressive mood and a player decides to get in the first blow, there's an outside chance he will sue for assault. It's a terrible situation, one you just can't win, and I'm thankful that the White Hart Lane incident is the only time I've been involved in a scuffle with a spectator.

One thing I've constantly had hurled at me is abuse, and some of the obscenities are really something. If anything, the language from the terraces – and some of the things I've been called – has got worse in recent years. It often makes me shudder to realize there are young children in the crowd listening to such diabolical language. It hardly promotes the image of football as a family game, for I wouldn't like my children to hear it.

An offshoot of the hooligan problem is that most League clubs now travel everywhere by coach, simply to avoid mixing with fans on railway stations and trains. More than once I've seen trouble on a platform after a game, with players being spat at or having a drink or a cup of hot tea thrown at them, ruining a suit or an overcoat. Some players naturally have a go back, but it's not easy in a crowd.

All the footballers I have met are totally disgusted by any form of hooliganism and at a loss to understand the reasoning behind it. Somehow you feel even worse about it when they are supporters of your own team. You want to disown those kind of fans – you need them like you need a hole in the head. Maybe they think that by a show of strength they are standing up for their own side. All they usually achieve is to prompt the same kind of reaction from opposing fans.

Sometimes you can be having a nice, quiet game – a good game – when the trouble erupts and, before you know it, there's extra tension on the pitch. I know it has often been claimed that a bad tackle, or a generally ill-tempered match, can start trouble on the terraces. I'm not saying it doesn't happen, yet nine times out of ten it isn't the players who start bother.

Even on the morning of a match, before a ball has been kicked, you see visiting fans on the rampage wrecking a place. Teenagers get tanked up on a coach or a train and it goes to their heads, but why they spend so much money and travel so far to get violent is baffling. It's absolutely mindless.

The picture I'm painting is not a pretty one, and it is not confined to Britain. There are plenty of continental hooligans.

Missile throwing started abroad, but it tends to be more dangerous in this country because our grounds are more compact. They help to provide genuine football atmosphere during a game, yet players – and especially goalkeepers – feel safer when there is a running track round a pitch, as is often the case abroad.

Not that distance alone is a guarantee of safety. I've never had any trouble at Wembley, but every now and again you read of a spectator running on during a game. And, of course, one or two England–Scotland matches have ended with the crowd swarming all over the pitch, and even digging lumps of it up. There again drink contributes to the situation, for I've heard it said the Scots do like an occasional dram.

I've seen a fair share of 'aggro' when playing abroad. Once it even came from an opposing player when Spurs went to Portugal and met Setubal in a European tie.

When the home side had a corner-kick and I moved off my line to attempt to catch the ball, a Setubal forward chucked a handful of dirt in my face and temporarily blinded me. I think I might have blown my top if a Spurs defender had not headed the ball away, but I just wrote it down to experience. Ever since, I've been on my guard not to get caught again.

Foreign spectators can be a menace. When Arsenal played in Turkey, against Fenerbache, we found ourselves in trouble on the morning of the match when we turned up at a local ground for training. There were hundreds of people waiting for us and when we walked through them two or three of the Arsenal lads were kicked and most of us were covered in spit.

I've another not-so-happy memory of Turkey when playing for Northern Ireland in an international match. As we left the field at the final whistle dozens of bottles rained down on us. The sound of those bottles breaking around our feet – fortunately, none of the players suffered more than a glancing blow – made us run for the cover of the dressing rooms like Olympic sprinters. It was what certain managers and coaches would call 'motivation', and it definitely motivated me.

It's odd how often I have seen trouble at pre-match training sessions like the one in Turkey. I think foreign fans hope to intimidate visiting teams in advance and unsettle them for the match. The same thing happened in Athens in September 1981 when Arsenal went to Greece for a UEFA Cup-tie against Panathinaikos. It seemed that those who turned up came to abuse us – without understanding the language, it wasn't hard to get the message – rather than watch the training session.

When you play in places like Greece and Italy, the fireworks which cascade down on to the pitch, often for the full 90 minutes, can make you a trifle nervous. You are never quite sure what they are made of, and whether it is safe to pick them up and clear your goalmouth in case they blow up. The same applies to smoke bombs with different coloured smoke pouring out. Your instinct is to kick them away, but you hesitate because you are frightened they might explode. I suppose it's the fear of the unknown.

Fireworks don't seem to worry continental players, presumably because they have become used to them, and I've been around enough not to bother too much. But youngsters who haven't previously played abroad tend to be apprehensive and I've known a few who found it hard to produce their usual form in all the noise.

There is no doubt about it that fans are better behaved behind the Iron Curtain, which is some consolation for the other kind of hassle you suffer in Eastern Europe where hotels and food are often not up to standard. Whether it is sheer discipline which keeps spectators in their place or fear of the kind of treatment they can expect from police, and officialdom, if they step out of line, I don't know. What I do know is that I've played in Russia several times without a hint of trouble on the terraces.

Russian spectators appear particularly appreciative of good football and are quick to applaud a skilful move by either side. And when Spurs played Dynamo Tbilisi, in Georgia, we were really made to feel welcome.

An estimated 5000 turned up just to see us train on the day before the game. It was a vast ground, open to the skies, and they stood around and clapped every good shot and gave me a big hand for each save. And they were just as fair during the game itself, even if a bit disappointed that we held Dynamo to a draw.

The snag about playing in Russia is that they insist upon making all the travel arrangements and that can double the time of the journey. You have to fly to Tbilisi via Moscow instead of going direct, and any British team arrives travel-weary.

West Ham suffered far more inconvenience than Spurs when they had a European Cup-winners' tie in Tbilisi in 1981, finding Moscow Airport snowbound when they arrived. As a result, the West Ham party spent hours in the airport and eventually had to stay overnight before completing the journey. Yet it could all have been avoided by a direct flight.

It was quite an achievement by West Ham to win the match 1–0, though the margin wasn't enough after losing the first game 4–1 to the Russians who went on to capture the cup.

My first season of European football at club level was 1967–68 when Spurs, having won the FA Cup the previous season by beating Chelsea 2–1 at Wembley, qualified for the Cup-winners' tournament. We went through the opening round smoothly enough, defeating Hajduk Split of Yugoslavia, and were then drawn against Olympique Lyons of France.

That proved to be the end of the road for Spurs, losing 1–0 in Lyons and going out of the competition on the away-goals rule after winning the return encounter 4–3 at White Hart Lane. Our team had been weakened by injuries and it was a farcical and unhappy finish when the French scored twice in the closing minutes after Spurs seemed to be coasting through to the next round. Manager Bill Nicholson was choked at the way we let the match slip, and I can't say I blame him.

My outstanding memory, though, is of the first game in Lyons because there was a mini-riot in which the crowd swarmed on to the pitch after an incident when Alan Mullery and one of the French players were sent off. They had gone down in a tangle and the Frenchman used his legs to prevent Alan getting back on his feet. Tempers became heated, blows were exchanged and the referee just didn't know what day it was as other players from both sides joined in. I tried to reach the spot where it was all happening with the intention of splitting them up, but I got only ten yards or so when I ran into a brick wall of fans as they raced on in their hundreds.

When the referee tried to sort things out, he gave Alan his marching orders but clearly wasn't sure about the identity of the Lyons player involved. That was when Alan Gilzean got into the act by pointing out the offender, who was promptly ordered off with Mullery.

That was in the first half. As we left the field at the interval, Alan Gilzean sensed the French player might be waiting for him in the tunnel – a huge cavern of a place used for cycle racing with dozens of doors leading to small dressing rooms. He decided to wait for me to walk with him, in the mistaken belief that I would afford him some protection. 'Hi, big man,' he said. 'Keep an eye on me in case that fellow is hanging about.' So I duly walked down the tunnel behind him, looking from side to side to see if anybody was lurking by one of the doors.

While I was glancing in one direction, I suddenly heard a scuffle and looked round just in time to see the French player landing one right on the point of Gilly's chin. Then Bill Nicholson suddenly appeared on the scene to separate them. Gilly wasn't amused. It was the last time I was ever called upon to act as a minder for any of the lads.

On my first travels, with Northern Ireland, it wasn't so much the fans as the referees who amazed me. They were totally biased towards the home teams because of the pressure from the crowd.

It might sound an easy thing to say, but some of the decisions were so outrageous that you felt you were playing against the referee, the fans and the home side all at once. It is something which has to be experienced to understand.

After a few trips I began to accept the situation more readily, putting it down to human nature: some of the referees were just plain scared of upsetting the crowd. Generalizations I know can be misleading, and I would count as an exception to this rule referees from behind the Iron Curtain. Perhaps they are more disciplined because of the system which breeds them, but certainly they never appear to be influenced so easily.

I'd like to include a referee on the list of the football folk I know well, but the truth is that I've never had much to do with a ref off the field. They are, of necessity, a distant breed.

I get on well with practically all of them during a game. I find if you are polite in your dealings with referees, they treat you in the same fashion. That's not to say I don't have a little moan when a corner-kick is awarded against me when I think it should be a goal-kick. But I learned my lesson one day when I shouted at a ref, 'Hey, that was a mistake!' He promptly replied, 'Well, you've made enough in your time.' A bit cruel, I thought, but I couldn't honestly argue.

Gordon Hill, now retired, was probably the referee who gained the respect of most players. Gordon was somewhat unorthodox in his methods: if a player swore at him he would swear back in a way which could make your hair curl. That style of tit-for-tat was OK, but I must admit I always thought it a trifle dangerous.

If a player swore at a referee in the next game, the chances were that he would get sent off for dissent. You have to know your man and just how far you can go when disputing a decision. Generally it's a pure waste of time, anyway.

I have always believed that it would be a benefit if more ex-footballers became referees, because of their awareness of the problems which players face. But I accept it isn't really practical as it takes time for a referee to graduate through the ranks from minor soccer to Football League status. And, let's be fair, the financial rewards wouldn't tempt many First Division stars.

I have a lot of admiration for referees, who are relatively poorly paid and clearly motivated in the first instance by their interest in the game. There might be one or two glory-seekers in the ranks, but the same applies to players and managers. All I know is that after being persuaded to referee the occasional charity match it's a thankless task, and I wouldn't relish the responsibility of having to make a vital decision in a crucial League match or a cup final at Wembley.

It's often debated whether British referees are better or worse than their foreign counterparts. My experience is that they are not so easily intimidated as the majority of continentals. I've played for Northern Ireland, Spurs and Arsenal teams who have been on the wrong end of some unbelievable decisions abroad when referees have been influenced by crowd pressure.

There has been an improvement in recent years, due in part to the appointment by FIFA and UEFA of neutral assessors who – in addition to noting match organization and crowd behaviour – have to report upon the performance of referees in European ties and international games.

Perhaps it's a coincidence, though I don't think so, that Arsenal have found life easier abroad when accompanied by Sir Stanley Rous – who is president of the club as well as being a former FIFA supremo and a world-famous figure in football. The very presence of Sir Stanley seems to guarantee the right balance of neutrality by any referee. He was a referee himself 50 years ago, before beginning his administrative career as secretary of the Football Association, and somehow I don't think I'd have dreamed of arguing with him.

8

BOUQUETS AND BRICKBATS

When I'm in reflective mood, my wife Eleanor is watching TV and the children have gone to bed, I flick through the pages of my scrapbook and relive the joys of good games and the agonies of the not-so-good ones. Like everybody else, I enjoy being praised and bristle a little when I'm criticized.

I'm lucky that over the years I've had more bouquets than brickbats. The press have been pretty good to me, and I think I have a good relationship with most of the leading soccer writers. Inevitably they exaggerate on occasions. The very nature of the media means that journalists see things in terms of black and white, so a footballer becomes accustomed to seeing his displays labelled 'tremendous' or 'terrible' when the truth is usually in the grey area between the two.

I have cuttings of articles headlined 'Jennings is the world's number one' and 'Jennings is the world's top goalkeeper'. That may well be overdoing it, but it's still very flattering and does the old ego a power of good.

I've forgotten most of the saves I've made. That's not false modesty, it's a cold fact. It isn't so surprising, either, when you remember just how many games I've played since the day I joined Watford more than 19 years ago. At the last count the total in League, various cup competitions and internationals was over 900 – when you add friendly fixtures and tour matches it must be well in excess of 1000.

So, with the odd exception, a save which delighted me at the time has faded from the memory. It is only when I'm chatting with friends or fans, and one of them says 'What about the day you stopped that shot from old So-and-so' that I have an action replay in my mind and the moment lives again.

People tend to remind you of your mistakes as well, and that's fair enough. Like every other goalkeeper I've been guilty of losing bad goals. I've been able to forget some of those, too, but one not so long ago will haunt me for the rest of my days.

It was, as you've probably already guessed, at my old stamping ground White Hart Lane on 2 January 1982 when Spurs beat Arsenal

1–0 in the third round of the FA Cup. Garth Crooks scored what must surely be the softest goal of his career in the first half to win that tie for Spurs. And I was entirely to blame.

Garth mishit his shot from just inside the penalty area, and to this day I couldn't tell you how or why the ball got past me. I've thought about it often enough, and I can only think that I took my eye off the ball to check if another Spurs player was following up. But, whatever the reason, it slithered under me and trickled into the net.

Everybody else in the ground must have been as surprised as I was, Crooks most of all. He had burst clear with enough room and time to get in a really good shot and I was praying he would put it wide or over the top, since the odds were so heavily stacked against me. Maybe it was partly my relief that Garth had made a mess of it that led to me making an even bigger blunder.

At the moment it happened I just wished the ground would open up and swallow me – and if that doesn't sound very original, I can assure you it's absolutely true. I lay awake for hours that night trying to work out how I could have been so stupid. It all seemed like a bad dream, but the newspaper headlines next morning soon reminded me it was a recurring nightmare. Especially as the BBC *Match of the Day* cameras had recorded it for posterity.

To happen at Tottenham of all places rubbed salt into the wound. It was so different from the first occasion when I returned to White Hart Lane as an Arsenal player, and we beat Spurs 5–0.

The thing which hurt most of all was that my Cup error cost Arsenal the match. If Arsenal had come back to win, or even equalized to force a replay and give us another chance, it would have been much easier to take and I could afford to smile about it and dismiss it as just one of those things. That's one of the penalties of being a goalkeeper. If you make a mistake which proves vital, you can't wipe it out even if you make a dozen brilliant saves in the same match. In the end it is the result which counts.

Terry Neill, Don Howe and the Arsenal lads took it well, despite what they must have been feeling. There were no accusing fingers pointed at me in the dressing room at half-time or at the finish. Most fellow professionals take the right attitude in such circumstances, because they know it could be their turn in the next game.

The only suggestion which hurt me when the post-mortems were conducted in the press was that I had other things on my mind during the game, because I had been involved in negotiations with Arsenal about a new contract during the previous week. Nothing could have been further from the truth. When an important match is in progress it demands one hundred per cent concentration, and there's not a single second when you can think about other matters.

As events turned out on that disastrous afternoon, the pain was physical as well as mental – 15 minutes from the end I tore a muscle in my groin when challenging Crooks after he had again got clear of our defence. I'd never believed in bogey-men before, but Garth made me revise that opinion.

I knew the damage was serious the moment I attempted my tackle on Garth, in an attempt to force him out of our penalty area and give a couple of our defenders time to get behind me and cover the goal. The muscular spasm was killing me, I could hardly move and I had to be helped from the field.

Our physio Fred Street wanted to call for a stretcher, but I wouldn't have it. Enough had gone wrong without being carried off feet first. I couldn't have endured the extra indignity.

It was the first time in my club career I had failed to finish a game so, on the law of averages, I suppose I couldn't complain. The only previous occasion I had ever missed any part of a match was in the Northern Ireland v England international at Windsor Park, Belfast, in October 1966. Then I was doubtful right up to kick-off time through injury, but it was decided I should take a chance and play. The handicap was too much and I only lasted the first half, with Willie McFaul taking over at the interval.

The groin tear at Tottenham, which added injury to insult, was slow to heal . . . I had far more time than I wanted to think about that Crooks goal. George Wood did his stuff in goal for Arsenal's first team while I struggled to get fit. It was more than seven weeks before I was ready, after three reserve outings, for a big match. Then I made my come-back not for Arsenal, but for Northern Ireland against England at Wembley. It wasn't a case of many happy returns, for England won 4–0.

It just proves to a player when his luck is right out. If I hadn't been hurt at White Hart Lane, I would have been in action twice a week afterwards and would have got that mistake out of my system even if the memory had lingered on.

They claimed during the war that the best therapy for a pilot who had been shot down was to get back into the air as soon as possible. The same goes for a footballer after a bad game. It worked that way for me after the worst mistake I made while playing for Spurs, when I let a shot through my legs against Manchester United at Old Trafford.

That was on a Saturday afternoon, but on the following Monday we had another First Division game at Blackpool and I had a blinder. I stopped everything which came my way and we won, so everybody instantly forgot my Old Trafford error.

My pal Cyril Knowles was involved in two goals I conceded, both at White Hart Lane, which had vastly different results. One was a joke, the other was anything but funny.

The 'pantomime' goal was in a home League game with Crystal Palace. Cyril was in possession on the left touchline, about 25 yards from me, when he came under pressure and decided the wisest course of action was a pass back. I realized what he had in mind and came off my line to make it simple for Cyril, when he completely misjudged the power of his intended pass and lobbed the ball way over my head and under the bar. Manager Bill Nicholson wasn't amused, but we finished 2–1 winners and the rest of the Spurs lads had a laugh about it afterwards.

It was not so funny on the night we were knocked out of the League Cup by Chelsea in 1972. It was the second leg of the semi-final and the aggregate scores were level with only a few minutes remaining when Chelsea's Alan Hudson tried a hopeful shot from an acute angle on the left byline. Cyril was well placed on the near post and there wasn't any danger as he swung his foot to attempt a mighty clearance.

I was looking up to the stand to see where Cyril had whacked the ball when, to my horror, it rolled under his foot and into the net. I was caught completely off balance and Spurs were out of the League Cup. Cyril took the brunt of the blame, but I had made the classic error of taking something for granted. Spurs won the trophy in both 1971 and 1973 and, but for that goal, might well have achieved a unique hat-trick – instead Chelsea beat Stoke at Wembley.

I have always been prepared to hold my hands up when I've boobed on any particular goal, or generally had a poor game. So I feel I've every right to resent criticism when I know it's not deserved. A case in point is the European championship qualifying match at Wembley when England beat Northern Ireland 4–0 (that score again!). I was blamed that night for two goals which were not my fault.

Kevin Keegan, who isn't exactly the biggest fellow in the world, scored the first with a header as I came out to challenge him – and the majority of the critics thought I should have got the ball. In fact, I did well to get so close to Kevin who was completely unmarked when the ball was crossed.

I could have stopped on the line and nothing would have been said, but that would have been cheating on myself. I realized the odds were against me, yet I thought that by flying out at Keegan I might distract him enough to prevent him making contact. As it happened he faltered for a split second, and didn't head the ball cleanly, but the touch he got was sufficient to turn the ball into the net.

Although it went wrong on the night, I'd do the same again tomorrow. It's not a goalkeeper's job to protect his own image. He must be ready to make himself look silly if he thinks it's in the interests of his team.

I also took some stick for England's fourth and final goal in that match when I failed to reach a cross. What the critics, the fans and – unfortunately – the referee didn't spot was Mick Mills running into my path and obstructing me. It was the neatest kind of professional foul and it worked a treat.

There have been quite a few red-letter days in my career that I remember with pride. But one date I'll never forget, for a very different reason, is Wednesday, 17 April 1968. That night at Elland Road, Leeds, my name went into a referee's notebook for the first and – so far – only time.

Since I've played in about 1000 first-class games, I suppose I can claim that my disciplinary record is pretty impressive. But I still get mad with myself when I recall how I was booked by Mr Peter Baldwin, though I honestly think I suffered extreme provocation.

Matches between Leeds and Spurs were never kid-glove affairs. Leeds in those days had an exceptionally good team and when we met there was no quarter asked or given. You had to be at your sharpest, for the Leeds lads under Don Revie were noted for their gamesmanship. In fact, I always got the impression they were proud of it.

The two clubs had clashed at White Hart Lane five days earlier on Good Friday, and Spurs had won to end an unbeaten Leeds run of 26 games. When we travelled up to Yorkshire we knew they would be seeking instant revenge for that set-back.

I certainly got a quick reminder, for a Leeds player ran into me on the first occasion I went to gather a cross from the wing – and that treatment was repeated five or six times in a tough but goalless first half. I accepted the knocks as part and parcel of the game, for my upbringing in Gaelic football in Northern Ireland had accustomed me to physical challenge. Yet by the interval I was beginning to feel Leeds were laying it on just a little thick.

Even so, I kept my cool until the 63rd minute when I jumped to fist the ball away and Leeds striker Mick Jones cannoned into me. We both crashed to the ground. The trouble started when I tried to regain my feet. Jones used his legs to keep me pinned to the turf for what must have been a few seconds, but seemed like ages.

When I eventually struggled free, we both jumped up and glared at each other. Mick must have thought I was going to have a swing at him and decided to get in first by planting a right-hander on my chin.

That was too much! I lashed out with my foot and kicked his behind. It was a natural reaction, even if a foolish one, and I was spotted by a linesman who instantly put up his flag to draw the attention of Mr Baldwin. By then the ball had gone out of play for a throw a fair distance up the field, but the referee not only booked me but added what I regarded as insult to injury by awarding Leeds a penalty.

The Spurs defenders who had seen the incident from the moment of impact between Mick and myself protested in vain, and skipper Dave Mackay was so incensed that when the ball was placed on the spot he kicked it into our net in a mixture of anger and frustration. Not that the delay did Spurs any good or unsettled Peter Lorimer, the Scottish international winger who had a reputation for his cannonball shot. Lorimer beat me all ends up with his penalty and that was enough for Leeds to win 1–0. It hardly cooled any Spurs tempers and ten minutes later another incident saw one of our star Scots, Alan Gilzean, sent off following a clash with Leeds full-back Terry Cooper.

I was upset. I'd never been booked before – not even in schoolboy or youth football – and being responsible for Spurs losing both points hardly made me feel any better.

The other players seemed to understand, but if I expected any sympathy from manager Bill Nicholson I soon discovered it wasn't forthcoming. Bill gave me a real rocket when I got back to the dressing room. He told me that Leeds' gamesmanship was no secret and that I should have known better than to rise to the bait.

I thought at the time, and I still do on reflection, that Bill was a bit harsh. He'd been sitting on the touchline and hadn't stopped one on the chin. But I learned my lesson the hard way and since that night I've always managed to turn the other cheek when I've been fouled. I admit I can take care of myself when under challenge in goalmouth scrambles, but I've never attempted to hurt an opposing player.

Perhaps I'm lucky to be blessed with a placid temperament, for it takes a lot to make me angry either on or off the field. Plenty of players who constantly get into trouble with referees just can't help reacting on the spur of the moment, even if they regret it immediately.

Even the fact that I gave away a penalty on that torrid night at Leeds was a rare happening. I have conceded very few over the years.

So far as Mick Jones was concerned there was no bad feeling between us once the final whistle had sounded – no confrontation in the tunnel or the start of a feud. He had the last laugh on that occasion, and I wrote it down to experience.

But, like many other people in the game who remember Leeds during the Revie era, I have often wondered if they sold themselves short by trying to be too clever; whether they might not have been even more successful if they had been a bit more loveable. I know the policy at Elland Road was to win points rather than friends but, believe me, the side was oozing with talent.

Johnny Giles and Billy Bremner were both great players who formed what was probably the finest mid-field partnership I've ever seen. And although Norman Hunter was noted for his reputation as a hard man he had tremendous skill, far more than most spectators probably realized.

Leeds also had a centre-half in Jackie Charlton who not only made life hard for opposing centre-forwards, but also became a goalkeeper's nightmare because of his ploy of coming upfield every time Leeds had a corner and positioning himself on the goal-line. When Jackie was in your path he wasn't an easy fellow to shift.

Most teams used to detail a striker to come back to mark Jackie whenever Leeds had a corner, which only added to the goalkeeper's problems by putting yet another body in an already crowded penalty area. Sometimes, the marker was as big a nuisance as Charlton, because he provided an extra obstruction when all a goalkeeper wants is a clear run at the ball.

Gordon McQueen, another powerful man, followed Jackie into the Leeds No 5 shirt and followed his example at corner-kicks as well. McQueen, an accurate header of a ball even when under pressure, has nodded more than one goal past me – both for Leeds and Manchester United.

I remember one instance not so long ago when Gordon came up for a Manchester United corner and Frank Stapleton, later to become his team-mate at Old Trafford, came back to help us deal with the threat. At least, that was Frank's intention – but he finished up impeding me as McQueen headed the ball home.

Don Howe was furious after the game, and blamed me for the goal. Don brushed aside my argument that I wasn't at fault because big Frank got in the way, but after he had seen the episode on television later that night Don was prepared to admit that maybe I had a point.

Mind you, he didn't go as far as to say that my version was right. That's not Don Howe's style. He's a bit like Bill Nicholson in that respect. Both have decided views of their own and don't encourage anything which sounds like an excuse from one of their players.

To go back to Leeds, you find the majority of players from other clubs don't relish a visit to Elland Road. Yet I've had some enjoyable games there and never had any complaints with the treatment I received from the fans.

My proudest moment at Leeds came in April 1978 when manager Terry Neill appointed me skipper of Arsenal for the first time, towards the end of my first season with the club. Pat Rice was injured and Terry presumably chose me because I was the oldest member of the team. The fact that I hadn't missed a single match that season probably influenced him as well.

Arsenal hadn't won at Elland Road in nearly 40 years, but we cracked it with a 3–1 victory. I didn't lead the players on a lap of honour, but when we reported for training the following Monday I kidded Pat Rice I was ready to make a takeover bid for the captaincy. He waited until we lost the next match, 1–0 at Liverpool, and then got his own back by telling the rest of the players that the responsibility was affecting my form.

I can't say that I have any lucky grounds, although I always enjoy a trip to Merseyside to play against Everton or Liverpool. I have made the occasional error at both Goodison Park and Anfield, but the atmosphere at both places invariably adds to the drama of any match.

Anfield will forever have a special spot in my memory because I saved two penalty-kicks in a 1–1 draw with Liverpool on Grand National Day, 1973. It was a morning match, so that the fans had time either to go on to Aintree or to have a quick lunch-time drink before watching the big race on TV.

Liverpool were chasing the League championship that season – as usual – and nobody gave Spurs much chance of avoiding defeat. But I had one of those days, the dream of every goalkeeper, when it seemed I could do no wrong. I was having a good season and, in fact, was voted as Footballer of the Year by the Football Writers' Association at the end of it, and I've no doubt my double penalty save helped me win the award.

Although those saves earned a great deal of publicity, it has to be admitted that neither was exactly in the super class. Kevin Keegan and Tommy Smith, who took the kicks, must both have been annoyed they didn't connect as cleanly as they intended. On each occasion I simply picked the right direction to go and stopped both shots without a great deal of bother. I made four or five better saves that morning which gave me considerably more satisfaction.

It was one of my lucky days, and the rest of the Spurs lads reckoned that if they could have found me a horse I'd have won the National. In fact, I didn't even back the winner.

That penalty performance was at least a consolation for me after a painful experience in an FA Cup replay at Anfield a few years earlier. I saved a Tommy Smith spot-kick in that game as well, but the referee ordered a re-take through no fault of mine. Spurs were making a substitution at the same time, and actually had 12 players on the pitch as I made my save. A linesman pointed out what had happened, and Tommy made no mistake the second time, Liverpool finishing the day as 2–1 winners.

Most of my trips to Midlands grounds have worked out quite well – though I have been on winning and losing sides at all of them in turn. The worst game of all was at the Baseball Ground, Derby, in Spurs' relegation season of 1976–77. We lost 8–2 and I can still picture the scene in our dressing room at the end with manager Keith Burkinshaw, clearly at a loss for words, sitting down with his head in his hands. If Keith took it badly, just imagine how I felt. I had never been beaten eight times in a game, and Spurs finished so demoralized it could have been ten or twelve.

It was the complete reverse to that heady day at Liverpool when I could do nothing wrong, for this time it seemed that every Derby scoring attempt eluded me. Spurs just fell to pieces: you could see our players dropping their heads and the Derby full-backs were coming upfield at regular intervals to get into the act.

My old pal Dave Mackay was Derby's manager at the time. He must have enjoyed a few drinks afterwards to celebrate such a runaway triumph. I just felt terrible. It was humiliating. Yet I had the consolation of knowing there wasn't anything I could have done to avert the rout. Perhaps on another day I might have stopped a couple of those Derby goals, but not one resulted from a glaring mistake on my part. All too often the Derby players were given the freedom of our penalty area with plenty of space to tee up scoring shots. Yes, on reflection, it could have been worse.

I have said that I've forgotten most of my saves, but one I was particularly proud of was from Liverpool's Steve Heighway at Anfield –

a ground where I've had my share of good games without ever finishing on the winning side. I know it must have been exceptional, for afterwards Steve was quoted as saying: 'Pat's save left me wondering how he had got to the ball. I burst through with half-a-dozen Spurs players behind me, and I had to shoot quickly. I really caught my shot just right, and it was going over Pat's right shoulder as he came out. I could hear the crowd behind the goal, stretching right up into the Kop, shouting "goal" – but there was the ball in Pat's hands. It was amazing. One of the finest saves I've seen in my life.'

Another which earned a great deal of praise was in a League Cup semi-final against Newcastle at White Hart Lane. The Newcastle build-up was perfect, with four or five passes strung together, before Tommy Craig hit a fantastic volley. But I was in the right place to hurl myself through the air and turn the ball over the top. Mike Bailey, of Wolves struck an equally fine volley from a corner-kick when playing against me at Tottenham and again I was able to turn the ball over the bar.

Those three saves, which earned accolades like 'best of the season', had something in common which had nothing at all to do with me. Heighway, Craig and Bailey all suffered because each, in turn, struck the ball perfectly and I was able to counter by going the right way and doing the right thing. If any had been mishit and screwed off the foot of the striker, I might well have been beaten.

There was another save at Wembley, when Arsenal lost 1–0 to Ipswich in the 1978 FA Cup final, which got a ten-out-of-ten rating. It was from a close-range header by full-back George Burley and I turned it for a corner. Afterwards I was asked how I managed to get to the ball, so I didn't like to tell anybody I thought I should have held it. There are times when silence is golden.

Each of the saves I've recalled were made easier because the ball was travelling through the air. Those at ground level are far more difficult, especially if the pitch has been churned up or is heavily sanded. I've been put on the spot more than once by a shot whipping off a sandy surface, and I'd rate sand as big a hazard as ice.

I've never worried in advance about facing any particular forward – even the most lethal like George Best, Bobby Charlton, Jimmy Greaves and Denis Law. All you end up with is an inferiority complex. I'm equally sure that none of those four ever gave a thought to the identity of an opposing keeper before a game. When you are mixing in the highest company, you win some and lose some.

Old Trafford is another Lancashire ground where I've had mixed fortunes. I scored my one and only goal there, in the 1967 FA Charity Shield in the days before the annual pre-season event was staged at Wembley, but I've conceded a few soft ones there myself.

In the mid-sixties it was something of an ordeal to play against United at Old Trafford. You had to be on your toes when facing an attack which included George Best, Bobby Charlton and Denis Law. Each one was a potential match-winner and all of them had me picking the ball out of the net on different occasions.

Charlton, in particular, was always a menace so far as I was concerned, beating me with thundering long-range drives. I reckon I would save some of those shots today, a feeling which grows stronger whenever I see a film clip of one of them. But Bobby seemed able to catch me in two minds when he let fly.

Maybe I'm kidding myself with the passage of time, and that if Bobby was playing now he would still be whacking them past me. After all, he scored goals all over Europe throughout his long and distinguished career and there can have been few more lethal marksmen in the history of the game.

Different strikers inevitably cause you different problems and before we became Arsenal team-mates, I had some fascinating duels with Malcolm Macdonald. Malcolm wasn't the most accurate finisher in the sense of picking his spot, but he could create a chance out of nothing because he had such electrifying pace. When he came bursting through you always knew Malcolm was going to blast the ball, and you just hoped you could get in the way or stick out an arm or a foot. One thing's for sure – if you stayed rooted to the line you had next to no chance.

It is when you come up against foreign teams that you step into the great unknown. There is an added touch of mystery to any free-kick the opposing side may get in your half of the field, and especially if it's within 30 yards of goal.

Most continental sides have a free-kick specialist who can swerve a ball round a defensive wall and a goalkeeper has to be on his toes. Even if you know what to expect it can be tricky. Dutch international Willie van Hanegem, who played for Feyenoord against Spurs in the 1974 UEFA Cup final, was as good as any I've ever faced.

Feyenoord also figured in my first-ever match on the continent, a few weeks after I had signed for Spurs. They beat us 4–3 in a pre-season friendly game in Rotterdam, and so dominated the proceedings that the final score flattered us.

Since then I've been three-quarters of the way round the world and I must have played in every European country from Iceland to Cyprus. Yes, even in Albania (in a World Cup qualifying tie for Northern Ireland) – not a place I'd put at the top of any holiday list.

The game I remember most of all was in Switzerland when I played for Spurs against Zurich Grasshoppers in a UEFA Cup-tie in September 1973. I don't think I've ever given a better display – yet, incredibly, Spurs won 5–1 that night.

It just shows how misleading a scoreline can be, for Grasshoppers outplayed us for long spells and could have had seven or eight goals. But my luck was in and I stopped everything except a first-half penalty by Adolf Noventa.

We were leading 2–0 at the time, from a couple of breakaway goals by Martin Chivers and Ray Evans, but the Swiss bombarded us non-stop after the interval. Finally they became so tired and frustrated that we wrapped it up with three goals in the last 12 minutes – one from Chivers and a couple from Alan Gilzean.

When we got back to the dressing room, Bill Nicholson told the other lads 'you ought to collect your bonuses and give the lot to Pat'. Coming from Bill that compliment was worth more than all the money in the Zurich bank vaults.

9

ON GOALKEEPERS AND GOALKEEPING

If I'm asked by friends what it feels like to be called the best goalkeeper in the world, I always reply that it's a lot better than being called the worst. Deep down I don't need telling that a goalkeeper, or any player, is as good as his last game.

The world is a big place, and in different countries they have different ideas about the standard of other people's goalkeepers. The English love to ridicule Scottish keepers and, like all generalizations, it is often unfair. Alan Rough, for instance, has suffered a great deal of unjustified criticism as a result.

But then not everybody else shares the high opinion the English have of their own goalkeepers. I was amazed to learn from Kevin Keegan that when he was playing in West Germany for Hamburg he found that a lot of Germans regarded English goalkeepers as a joke. Kevin didn't mention the Irish, yet I had an uneasy suspicion that I might have been included in that sweeping statement.

I've heard the theory advanced that foreign keepers have an easier life because nowhere do top clubs play as many games in a season as we do in England. But continental goalkeepers have to perform in more difficult conditions, with rock-hard grounds rattling your bones each time you hit the deck. Give me the softer pitches of Britain any day.

I certainly rate two continentals among the finest keepers I've ever seen – Sepp Maier of Bayern-Munich and West Germany and Dino Zoff of Juventus and Italy. As an old-timer myself, it's heartening that both enjoyed some of their greatest successes when in their thirties.

There was a feeling in Britain that Maier, whose career was eventually ended by injuries received in a car accident, wasn't all that hot – see what I mean about different opinions? – and that he was a lucky goalkeeper. Don't knock luck, it's important. But you need a lot more than good fortune to win as many medals as Maier. He helped Germany win the World Cup and the European championship and Bayern-Munich to complete a hat-trick of European Cup victories. No other goalkeeper has ever matched that remarkable record.

Maier was a master of positional play, and probably had his most memorable match in the 1974 World Cup final when the Germans beat the Dutch 2–1 in Munich. He made some marvellous saves that afternoon. Yet his greatest contribution was that he never made any costly mistakes throughout the entire competition – he was a model of consistency from beginning to end.

The first time I saw Zoff was when Juventus met Arsenal in the semi-final of the European Cup-winners' tournament in 1980. He was 38 by then, and he was absolutely magnificent in the first leg at High-bury. I stood at the other end and marvelled at his performance, not only his shot-stopping but the way he dealt with crosses and his overall command of the goalmouth.

According to Italian critics, Zoff was past his best at that time. All I can say if that is true is that I'd liked to have seen him in action five or ten years earlier, for watching him that night I appreciated just now good he must have been at his peak.

My admiration for Zoff grew when he helped Italy win the 1982 World Cup in Spain at the age of 40. It gave me hope as well, for I'd like to think I'm around for the next one in 1986 when I've passed the 40 mark.

Zoff, and Gylmar of Brazil, are the only goalkeepers to have made 100 international appearances for their country, but I have my fingers crossed I will reach that target. I've already reached 95 and would have passed the century but for occasional injuries and priority of club commitments. For 15 years my place was seldom in doubt, yet I never took my selection for granted or regarded myself as an auto-matic choice for Northern Ireland. Right through my career I have always felt that if I had a bad game I would be out, and every match could be my last. The gap between international fixtures adds to the possibility, particularly if you've let in three or four goals in the previous game. It's always easy to blame a goalkeeper for a heavy defeat.

Sometimes I've been asked if I have ever wished I was English. The answer is definitely not. The main reason is that I'm proud of being Irish. Another consideration is that although England probably play twice as many games as Northern Ireland, I would never have earned so many caps. Don't forget I was only 18 when I was first plunged into international football. I wouldn't have even been con-sidered by England at that time with Gordon Banks in his prime, and the presence of Peter Shilton and Ray Clemence would have been a double obstacle in more recent years.

I was thrilled when Sir Alf Ramsey picked me for the Wembley

In training for the ballet at Tottenham. (Keystone)

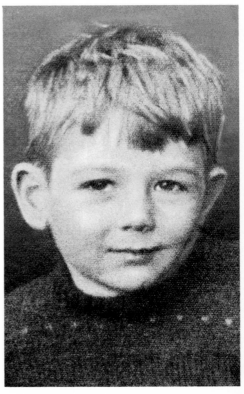

ABOVE A Spurs team line-up
with a difference, after my
marriage to Eleanor in January
1967: *left to right* Terry Venables,
Alan Mullery, Eddie Clayton,
Jimmy Robertson, Maurice
Norman, P.J., Eleanor, Ron
Henry (behind Eleanor), Phil
Beal, Bill Brown, Cliff Jones,
Dave Mackay, Cyril Knowles,
Jimmy Greaves, Frank Saul.
(Keystone)

RIGHT P.J. as a youngster.

Proud father of four. ABOVE
Siobhan, Ciára and Mairead
try on my Irish caps for size.
(Eric Huxtable) RIGHT Patrick
at five days old. (Monte Fresco/
Syndication International)

ABOVE Parading through the streets of north London after winning the 1967 FA Cup final. Cyril Knowles, Mike England and I look on as Alan Mullery and captain Dave Mackay hold the Cup aloft for the Spurs fans. (Central Press)

LEFT A crucial save in our 2-1 Wembley victory over Chelsea. (Sport & General)

ABOVE After beating Aston Villa in the 1971 League Cup final, Spurs' entry into Europe was marked by winning the UEFA Cup in 1972. Sharing in the celebrations after our victory over Wolves are assistant manager Eddie Baily, manager Bill Nicholson and trainer Johnny Wallis.
(Carleton Photographic)

RIGHT Martin Peters and I with Spurs' third trophy in three seasons – the 1973 League Cup.
(Carleton Photographic)

Two memorable saves at Anfield, one of my luckiest grounds. TOP The second of two penalties I saved against Liverpool on 31 March 1973, Tommy Smith being the unlucky striker in this one. (Provincial Press Agency)

BOTTOM Despite stopping Emlyn Hughes's spot-kick on 22 September 1973, there were twelve Spurs players on the field at the time and the kick had to be retaken. Unfortunately, I was not to repeat my March performance. (Syndication International)

TOP LEFT Receiving the 1973 PFA Player of the Year award. TOP RIGHT One of the more unusual moments in my career, when the ball burst during a game against my old club Spurs in December 1979. (Monte Fresco/Syndication International)

BOTTOM A victorious Arsenal team after beating Manchester United 3-2 in the 1979 FA Cup final: *back row* Walford, Price, P.J., Young, Sunderland, O'Leary, Stapleton and Rix; *front row* Brady, Rice, Nelson and Talbot. (Associated Press)

TOP The Northern Ireland line-up against Yugoslavia in the 1982 World Cup: *left to right* Martin O'Neil, Gerry Armstrong, Jimmy Nichol, Norman Whiteside, Sammy McIlroy, Billy Hamilton, Mal Donaghy, Dave McCreery, John McClelland, Chris Nichol, P.J. (Belfast Telegraph)

BOTTOM A tense moment during Northern Ireland's 1-0 victory over host-nation Spain. (Colorsport) match which marked Britain's entry into the Common Market, for I was chosen in front of Shilton and Clemence, who rate as exceptional goalkeepers in my book. Both have their own particular strengths and can be unbeatable on any given afternoon.

Shilton's handling is immaculate. He has a brilliant pair of hands, lightning reflexes and incredible agility for such a thickset man. Allied to his natural ability, which was evident from an early age, has been the countless hours he has spent training. He has worked harder than any other goalkeeper I know to maintain his own sky-high standards.

His determination is such that Shilton did not allow set-backs at club level – he was with both Leicester and Stoke when they were relegated – to affect his international form. No one was happier than me when Peter finally got among the medals with Nottingham Forest in the European Cup (twice), League championship and League Cup.

Clemence had the bonus of being with a more successful club, and picked up just about every honour that was going at Liverpool. He had to deal with a different kind of pressure with Liverpool constantly chasing the big prizes, thus making every game vital. I still find it hard to believe that Ray conceded only 16 goals in 42 First Division matches when Liverpool won the title in 1978–79. Only another goal-keeper could appreciate that achievement.

Clemence has the perfect build and agility is also his strong point. He developed in the Liverpool style as part-goalkeeper, part-sweeper by the goals he prevented by dashing from his line – a tactic essential when operating behind a square-playing defence. It may look risky at times, but Ray usually made it look simple because of his quick brain and supreme confidence.

It has been said that Shilton and Clemence are unfortunate to be contemporaries, that either would have reigned unchallenged if the other had not been around. I think it is the other top-class English goalkeepers who have been unlucky to find their international paths blocked by two men of such calibre.

Joe Corrigan immediately springs to mind. I can also think of Alex Stepney, who at his peak was the equal of any goalkeeper in the land, plus Phil Parkes and Jimmy Rimmer. I have the highest regard for all of them.

Rimmer must have thought he had made his England break-through in the summer of 1976 when selected as second string to Clemence – in the absence of Shilton – for a three-match tour of the United States to play in a competition against Brazil, Italy and the

USA. Rimmer was picked for the first half of the game with the Italians in New York, with Corrigan standing by to replace him at the interval.

Italy dominated the opening 45 minutes and led 2–0 at half-time, but England staged a second-half revival to win 3–2. The result was that Corrigan subsequently became a regular member of the England squad as third choice behind Clemence and Shilton. Big Joe was in the right place at the right time while Jimmy dropped out of the international reckoning. It shows how fate can take a hand.

If I had to nominate my number-one it would be Gordon Banks. I always had the impression he could go on forever. If it wasn't for the fact that he virtually lost the sight of one eye in a car crash I am sure he would have played until he was 40, like Zoff.

He was a superb goalkeeper, the ultimate 'Mr Reliable'. Gordon made mistakes like the rest of us, yet they were few and far between and he never allowed an error to shake his composure for the remainder of the game. He worked hard at his game and always made everything look so easy.

Gordon was a key man in England's 1966 World Cup triumph, keeping clean sheets for the first four matches and only being beaten by Eusebio's penalty in the 2–1 semi-final win over Portugal. He had a marvellous tournament and it speaks volumes for the Germans that they managed to score twice against him in the final.

Banks is best remembered for a remarkable save from Pelé in the 1970 World Cup. It was an incredible change of direction which made it possible and the action replay must have been screened thousands of times on television all over the world. Yet I'm sure Gordon would tell you that he made saves every bit as good during training sessions. That's when most goalkeepers pull off their most spectacular stops, unseen by the fans and without a camera in sight. Instead of headlines the only thing you get is personal satisfaction.

Usually when a young goalkeeper gets into the first team he is compared unfavourably with his immediate predecessor. At Tottenham it wasn't the man I replaced, Scottish international Bill Brown who had starred in the 'double' side, who haunted me, it was Ted Ditchburn, the idol of the fans when he kept goal for Spurs from the early war years until the late fifties.

I didn't see Ted play, but before I had the pleasure of meeting him I used to hate the very mention of his name. It was 'Ditchburn this' and 'Ditchburn that', and the odd condescending 'you're doing well son, but you'll never be another Ditchburn'. His popularity so long after he had left the club was amazing. I knew he must have been some goalkeeper.

It became a bit of a complex with me – until the day I was introduced to the great man himself. Almost the first words Ted said to me were, 'You are a better goalkeeper than I was.' I have my doubts – anyway, how can you compare players from different eras? – but I must admit it was music to my ears. It was typical of Ditchburn that he should make a rare return to White Hart Lane to present me with a club award when I passed his record League appearances for Spurs.

Because there was no *Match of the Day* when I was a youngster in Ireland – just the occasional clip from an important game on TV – I didn't get the opportunity to make a regular study of star goalkeepers. But I went along to Windsor Park to see Northern Ireland play whenever I got the chance and if I tried to model myself on anybody it was big Harry Gregg. He was something of a folk hero in Belfast because of his exploits with Manchester United and his excellent performances for Ireland in the 1958 World Cup.

Harry was a fine goalkeeper, a strong agile fellow who commanded his penalty area. I noted everything he did, but most of all I was impressed with his courage in withstanding physical challenge from opposing forwards. I admired the way he made up his mind and wasn't scared to come off his line if he thought the situation demanded it.

When I got my first cap for Northern Ireland it was, ironically, to replace Harry, who had carried the can for an 8–3 defeat by England at Wembley in the previous match some months earlier. Eight goals? It had to be the goalkeeper's fault.

In a way, succeeding Harry was like filling Ditchburn's boots at Tottenham, because he was so highly regarded by the rest of the Irish players. The older members of the team still liked to talk about his feats in the 1958 World Cup when Northern Ireland reached the quarter-finals and Harry was voted the outstanding keeper in the tournament.

The story was often told how, in one game, wing-half Tommy Casey had a go at Harry for making a mistake – and was promptly offered the goalkeeper's jersey by the irate Gregg and instructed to put it on if he thought he could do better. Tommy declined the offer.

After hanging up his boots, Harry had spells as a manager with several clubs in the lower divisions and then became a specialized coach of goalkeepers. I wish I'd had the benefit of his advice, and experience, when I was starting out instead of having to learn the hard way from my own mistakes.

Managers are seldom ex-goalkeepers so they tend to lack the practical know-how of how to deal with the problems which arise for a youngster. And, human nature being what it is, he rarely gets much help within his own club from a senior keeper who, understandably, senses a threat from a newcomer to his own position and livelihood. Peter Shilton has said that he never received any coaching from Gordon Banks when he was at Leicester; and when I joined Spurs I was never told by Bill Brown what I was doing wrong.

These days I'm glad to say most big clubs pay greater attention to coaching goalkeepers. Gordon Banks, as well as Harry Gregg, has utilized his vast experience in this way, while former Arsenal and Scotland keeper Bob Wilson supervises twice-a-week sessions at Highbury – or, rather, at the London Colney training ground.

Bob has helped me as well as George Wood and Paul Barron (who moved on to Crystal Palace). But it's young Rhys Wilmot who has probably reaped the major benefit from the experience of others, for, in addition to training, members of the Arsenal 'goalkeeper club' talk amongst ourselves about how to cope with certain situations which arise during a match.

I have never found coaching manuals much use. On the contrary, the 'advice' they contain is often misleading and some of the pet theories about goalkeeping are wide of the mark.

One widely held belief is that a goalkeeper should always stop a shot from outside the penalty-area if he has a clear view of the ball and the opponent striking it. All I can say is that there must be a lot of bad keepers in the game if you consider how many goals are scored from 20 or 30 yards' range, not only in League football but in international and World Cup matches.

There might have been a grain of truth in that argument in the days of the old leather ball. A lot of present-day forwards wouldn't have been capable of shifting it 30 yards in the first place. But the ball now in use is made of synthetic material with a polished surface. It's a nightmare for goalkeepers, for at times it is like trying to handle a bar of soap. If you lose just one per cent of your concentration it can squirm out of your grasp. The leather ball was much heavier and if you had a strong pair of hands and got your body behind it there was no danger. And it didn't play tricks by swerving wildly in flight. Nowadays you often start to go one way, only to find the plastic ball has changed direction.

That's why even the finest goalkeeper can be beaten all ends up by a long-range drive which has been struck with pace and accuracy. Just because you know where it is going doesn't mean you can prevent it getting there.

There is another widely held belief that every ball inside the six-yard area 'belongs' to the goalkeeper and he's at fault if he fails to collect it. That's cockeyed as well, for it all depends on the height and the angle at which the ball is played towards you – and on how many bodies are in the way. The goalkeeper used to be encouraged to station himself on the far post for a corner. If he tries it now there's a fair chance of being obstructed fifty per cent of the time because he hasn't a clear path to move forward if the ball only travels to the near post.

Some coaches believe there is an invisible barrier six yards out which inhibits keepers from coming any further. I've never been afraid to come off my line, but experience teaches you there's a time to do it and a time to stay.

If one of my defenders is close enough to an opposing forward to put in a decisive tackle, I'll let him get on with the job while positioning myself in case the challenge fails. By racing out too far you risk the merest touch, or a deflection, sending the ball into the net.

Should an opponent burst clear unchallenged it depends upon the speed at which the ball is moving whether you race from the line. Only a Pelé can chip a fast-moving ball, most players belting it with all their might. So the best tactic is to get as close as you can. If the ball is travelling at medium pace, and especially if it bounces near to the on-coming forward, it is risky to advance too far from the goal as you give the forward the scope to lift the ball over your head.

My method of spreading myself feet first when challenging a forward has been criticized by those who prefer a keeper to dive headlong in an attempt to smother the ball with his hands. My answer is that I'm giving myself time and space to react if the forward tries to shoot on the run, and it's easier to get up quickly if you need a second 'bite' to try and stop him. I'm not frightened of being kicked in the head, I just refuse to commit myself totally by diving towards an opponent and offering him the chance of side-stepping and taking the ball round me.

I suppose it's a case of doing what comes naturally, but I discount the text-books which insist my way is wrong. I feel I've proved my point on countless occasions. Bill Nicholson, when Spurs manager, agreed with me. He knew the value of trying to hold up an opponent who was bearing down on goal. He felt it was the duty of defenders to get back and cover every angle the moment I came off the line.

It may sound like stating the obvious, but the main priority of any keeper is to stop the ball. Whether he catches it, turns it over the bar or round a post may depend upon his individual style and the way he reads a certain situation. But it must always be first things first. The temptation to decide what you will do with the ball before it's in your hands can be dangerous. Accurate distribution is an important part of a goalkeeper's job, yet it is still secondary to keeping the ball out of the net. Thinking a couple of moves ahead is costly if, through inexperience, you take your eye off a ball travelling towards you. I've been caught napping like every other keeper.

A proportion of goals result from deflections by defenders or shots hitting divots and changing direction. But most of all you have to safeguard against an opponent miskicking. A mishit shot is the one most likely to finish in the bottom corner of the net after you have prepared yourself to deal with a power drive. And, believe me, First Division stars miskick like schoolboys sometimes, even if they don't always admit it. More than once I have seen the scorer of a vital goal go on TV after a game and explain, tongue in cheek, how he 'bent' the ball past me when we both knew he intended his shot to go into the opposite corner.

One comforting thought in my old age is that goalkeepers get far more protection from referees these days than they did when I was starting in League football. Any strong physical challenge by an opponent is usually penalized, whereas once you were more likely to end up with sore ribs than a free-kick.

I'm grateful for the change in attitude, even if I'm bound to say that it has probably robbed the fans of a degree of excitement and drama. Spectators used to relish the old goalmouth clashes, when wingers swung the ball across and the centre-forwards clattered everything and everybody in sight.

Alec Dawson, a powerful Scot who played for Manchester United and Preston, was the toughest fellow I ever met. I still have painful memories of one FA Cup-tie when I was at Tottenham when Alec knocked me over so often I began to wonder if it was worth getting up.

I'd learned the hard way in the Third Division with Watford where I came up against a succession of tough strikers. Billy McAdams was a fellow Irishman who showed me no mercy, while Coventry had both centre-forward George Kirby and centre-half George Curtis. The pair of them made each corner-kick an ordeal – if one didn't get you, the other surely would.

At least I avoided Bobby Smith. From what I later heard from Spurs team-mates, he ate goalkeepers for breakfast. If only half the stories about Bobby's exploits were true, I'm surprised some of the opposing keepers even turned up at White Hart Lane.

It was all part of the game, and I didn't mind it too much. I didn't expect any favours, and I had been well equipped for physical battles in my schooldays when I played Gaelic football which is best described as a cross between soccer and Rugby. It is not a sport for the faint-hearted and to survive you have to be able to give and take knocks without complaining. If you scare easily you don't play Rugby – and you don't even watch Gaelic football.

I used to play in mid-field and I was quite useful. I was on the fringe of a place in the County Down minor representative side when I turned my attention to soccer. That automatically barred me since the GAA – the Gaelic ruling body – did not approve of 'foreign' games.

Gaelic still proved the best preparation I could have had for soccer, even if I didn't realize it at the time. Not only is it a game where you are under constant pressure, and have to withstand knocks, but all the time you are leaping to catch the ball against opponents who are also using their hands. The result was that I developed safe handling while under challenge, and, looking back, it probably taught me to catch the ball one-handed – which has been useful to me even if it might appear a trifle showy when I do it in a First Division match.

It also helped my kicking, for in Gaelic football you have 50-yard free-kicks and at 14 I could usually get that distance, and, in open play, you had an advantage if you could kick the ball with either foot. When I arrived at Watford, my ability to drop-kick well into the opposing half of the field with right or left foot caused quite a stir.

While I know it isn't much help to a lad from any other country, I would urge any budding young Irish goalkeeper to spend at least a year playing Gaelic football. There's a lot of satisfaction to be derived from it, although nothing more tangible because it is a strictly amateur sport, and it will do him more good than any orthodox coaching.

One goal I have on my video at home is a bit special. It's certainly spectacular and it is most definitely a freak. Nobody knows that better than me – because I was the scorer.

It happened on a sunny August afternoon in 1967 during the FA Charity Shield match between Cup-winners Spurs and League champions Manchester United at Old Trafford. Those who later named United keeper Alex Stepney as the most surprised man in the ground got it wrong. That title belonged to me.

We had been awarded a free-kick just outside our penalty-area and

I shouted for the ball to be played to me, so that I could thump it up-field in the hope of reaching Alan Gilzean whom I'd spotted in an onside position about 25 yards from the United goal. I kicked; Alex started to advance from his line as the ball soared towards Gilzean, so that he could win the race if Alan didn't reach the ball or if it bounced clear as he tried to control it. Instead it dropped between the pair of them and in one bounce on the bone-hard surface went over the head of Alex into the net.

Everything seemed to go quiet, especially at the Stretford End where the United fans could hardly believe their eyes. I was a bit dazed and thought 'What happens now?' I wasn't sure if a goal would be awarded, so I didn't give any clenched-fist salute. Even the referee appeared to hesitate before deciding it must be a goal. Not one of the other Spurs players came rushing to congratulate me. Most of them just looked in my direction as if to say 'lucky blighter'.

I've never brought up the subject with Alex Stepney as I have some idea of how embarrassing it must be to him. I'm only glad the goal enabled us to draw 3–3, with both clubs holding the Charity Shield for six months, because in the same match I was beaten by a 30-yarder from Bobby Charlton which went in straight over my head. And I've never come close to repeating that feat, although I have often sent drop-kicks out at the other end after one bounce. They've all finished up in the crowd instead of in the back of the net.

I must say I enjoyed the experience of scoring that goal more when it became a talking point after the game, because it's always nice to achieve something out of the ordinary. It is not unique, of course, since Peter Shilton scored in similar circumstances in a League match at Southampton. Phil Parkes came close to joining the same exclusive club when he was with Queen's Park Rangers. He beat the opposing keeper with a drop-kick, only for the goal to be disallowed because a team-mate was standing in an offside position.

I remember seeing a TV clip of a Dutch League game when a goal-keeper raced upfield when his side were awarded a free-kick in the closing minutes. He positioned himself perfectly and was only inches away from glory with a header which rattled against the bar. The temptation to try something like that has nagged at me over the years. More than once I've wanted to have a go when my side has forced a corner when we were a goal down with five minutes or so left to play. I don't see there is much to lose, and I believe I could outjump anybody because of my natural spring. I'm not saying I'd score, but I might be able to knock the ball down for a team-mate.

You don't need to tell me that my manager and coach would go berserk. Even if I managed to score, I'm sure any instant praise would be coupled with a firm warning not to do it again.

There have been instances of goalkeepers actually playing in other positions in League football. Welsh international Johnny King, of Swansea, once had a couple of months at centre-forward and knocked in a few goals. And Gorden Nisbet made a permanent switch to full-back after making his First Division debut as a goalkeeper while at West Bromwich. Gordon couldn't get a regular first-team spot in goal, but was persuaded to try his luck at full-back. He was so successful that he has since totalled more than 400 League and Cup games with West Bromwich, Hull City and Plymouth Argyle. His side has the added bonus of having a spare keeper in any emergency.

When I was with Spurs, both manager Bill Nicholson and my club-mate Steve Perryman said they thought I was a sufficiently good all-round athlete to have made the grade in an outfield role. Who knows? Perhaps Bill and Steve were just being kind. But I think I would have had a chance of making the grade as a centre-half.

That probably explains why I get a kick from running outside my penalty-area to check an opposing raid by heading the ball away. I don't try it too often, but I never hesitate if I feel it's the correct thing to do. Once, against Everton at Goodison Park, I was no more than five yards from the half-way line when I headed the ball on to one of my defenders. I daren't look at our bench to see the reaction, but at least I got a big round of applause from the fans.

The important thing when a goalkeeper goes beyond his own 'box' is not to panic. If the ball is on the ground and I know I have enough time, I always look to pass to a team-mate instead of kicking it wildly anywhere. Once, during the FA Cup semi-final marathon between Arsenal and Liverpool which went to four games in 1980, I played a neat one-two with Willie Young before we cleared the ball.

It may have looked a bit cheeky, but I knew exactly what I was doing. Arsenal coach Don Howe wasn't so sure, for afterwards he told me I should have belted the ball into the crowd. I disagreed with Don. He wouldn't have expected another player to kick the ball into the stand. The trouble is that inside the game coaches and other players don't think that goalkeepers can 'play'. We are just there to use our hands but can't be trusted to kick or head the ball with any accuracy. I regard that kind of generalization as daft.

Being a good goalkeeper may call for different skills, but you need a quick brain and plenty of confidence to shine in any position. It is interesting to note that the most talented outfield players never shirk taking over in goal.

Tottenham's Glenn Hoddle has kept goal efficiently on more than one occasion after his keeper was injured. Glenn even survived extra time without conceding a goal when Spurs won 1–0 against Manchester United in an FA Cup-tie at Old Trafford.

Another Spurs and England star with natural skills who could do a sound job in goal was Martin Peters, while Jimmy Greaves was always hoping to get the opportunity to try his hand between the posts in a League game. Jimmy often turned out in Sunday charity games as a keeper while at White Hart Lane. And what about former England skipper Bobby Moore, who went into goal during a League Cup semi-final replay with Stoke City after Scottish international Bobby Ferguson was hurt? Moore stopped a penalty, but was unlucky enough to be beaten by the rebound.

Hoddle, Peters, Moore. You might think all three were too valuable in their normal roles to act as emergency keeper. But the secret is that they had the confidence as well as natural athletic ability. They also had that sixth sense which enables top players to read a game, to anticipate what is going to happen before it does. That is essential for a goalkeeper, and I like to think it's one of my strong points.

I never indulge in spectacular saves if I think I can avoid the need in the first place by anticipating the run of play and going out to collect the ball. By hesitating and letting in an opposing forward for a shot, in the hope that you will be able to stop the ball, you only make the job twice as difficult.

Study Peter Shilton or Ray Clemence for 90 minutes during a match and you'll end up surprised by how few saves they have to make – simply by doing the routine things well and catching shots which would bring desperate diving saves from lesser goalkeepers. Peter and Ray would both back me in saying prevention is always better than cure.

10

WEMBLEY

So many star footballers go right throughout their careers without getting the chance to play in a Cup final at Wembley – Bill Nicholson has told me how much he regrets the opportunity never came his way – that I regard myself as unbelievably lucky to have played in no fewer than six. So far as I'm aware, only my ultimate successor at Tottenham, Ray Clemence, has ever topped that total.

I figured in FA Cup-winning sides with Spurs in 1967 and Arsenal in 1979; in two successful League Cup teams for Spurs in 1971 and 1973; and was twice on the losing end with Arsenal in the FA Cup in 1978 and 1980.

Appearing at Wembley is always something special, but a Cup final is extra-special. It's a fantastic experience and, to me, there is always a far greater sense of occasion than playing there in an international match. This might be because the publicity build-up lasts so much longer – it is almost frightening by the time you get to the day.

You forget all the pre-match pressure when the whistle sounds to actually start the game, but you are still conscious of being watched on television by millions of people around the world who will get a close-up of any error you make. I was as much aware of that feeling in my sixth final as I was in my very first when Spurs beat Chelsea 2–1.

That day in 1967 was memorable for me for all kinds of reasons. Most important for Spurs was the fact that the 'new' side had finally won something for the first time since the break-up of the great team captained by Danny Blanchflower a few seasons earlier.

By the time we faced Chelsea we were bubbling with confidence as the result of an unbeaten run which stretched back more than four months. In addition to taking us to Wembley it had lifted Spurs from a mid-table spot in the First Division to a final position of third, only goal-average being the difference between us and runners-up Nottingham Forest. Everybody in the Spurs team knew we had the beating of Chelsea, and we won more comfortably than the scoreline reflected.

Every winning Cup side has a touch of fortune along the way, even if it has faded from the memory by the time they are celebrating at

Wembley, and Spurs were no exception that year. Our narrow squeak came right at the beginning of the Cup run, in a third-round tie away to Millwall – then a Second Division club – at the Den. It ended in a goalless draw, much to our relief, but in the last couple of minutes full-back Cyril Knowles cleared the ball off the line when I was well beaten.

We had a heck of a struggle to win the replay 1–0 at White Hart Lane before getting through the next two rounds with home victories over Portsmouth (3–1) and Bristol City (2–0). There were a couple of scares in the match with Bristol City, who failed to score with a twice-taken penalty, but the thing which sticks in my mind was a remarkable incident involving our captain Dave Mackay which might well have cost us the game.

In the early stages Dave was penalized for a foul on City's Bobby Kellard. It didn't look particularly bad, yet the referee pointed to the dressing room and we all thought Mackay had been sent off. Even to this day I believe that was the referee's intention, but Dave stood his ground and argued his case to such good effect that he remained on the field. If the red card had been in use at that time it might have been impossible to convince the ref to change his mind.

The quarter-finals involved us in another backs-to-the-wall fight on Second Division soil at Birmingham City's ground at St Andrew's. Again we drew 0–0, but then really hit the jackpot in the replay with a runaway 6–0 win. So we were through to the semi-finals and I had conceded just one goal in six ties.

In the semi-finals we were paired with Forest, who were chasing the League and FA Cup double at that stage. On the day of the match, at Hillsborough, Sheffield, I was more nervous than I have ever been in my life. Most of my family and many of my friends had come over from Newry, and it was as much as I could do to speak to them before the kick-off.

It wasn't Forest who put the wind up me, merely the thought of getting within one game of Wembley and then missing out. Any player who has been that close will tell you that losing a semi-final is the most shattering experience in football. Can you remember which two clubs were beaten in last season's semis?

The fear of defeat is that much greater in the FA Cup than in any other competition, for in the League Cup and in Europe the semi-finals are staged on a home-and-away basis. In the FA Cup you only get one chance.

In the event, I needn't have worried as Spurs beat Forest 2–1 and

Dave Mackay had a marvellous game. He had set his heart on climbing the Wembley steps to receive the Cup – Danny Blanchflower had been skipper in Spurs' two previous final triumphs in 1961 and 1962 – and nothing was going to stop him.

Forest coach Tommy Cavanagh, who believes in motivating his players with a show of confidence, had been quoted before the game as saying 'Spurs would be crushed like grapes'. So none of us were surprised when Mackay did his Churchillian act afterwards by seeking out Cavanagh and declaring 'Some grapes!'

I enjoyed the train ride back from Hillsborough to London, but I soon found the pressure was only just starting with the Cup final looming up, And most of it came from Newry.

Ten years earlier another local lad, Peter McParland, had brought glory to the town when he starred in an FA Cup final by scoring both goals in Aston Villa's 2–1 win over Manchester United. It was a match loaded with controversy, for in the first half Peter had collided with United goalkeeper Ray Wood who was so badly hurt he had to hand over his jersey to centre-half Jackie Blanchflower. There were no substitutes in those days, and the unfortunate Wood tried to struggle along on the wing for as long as he could.

McParland was the toast of Newry, and I idolized him as much as the rest of the kids – especially as Peter lived in the next turning to me in Upper Chapel Street. As a schoolboy he had also played in the same street team, 'Shamrock Rovers', where I was later to make my start.

There was terrific excitement in Newry when Peter played in that 1957 Cup final. I watched the game on my aunt's TV set and most of the people who owned televisions could have sold tickets, so great was the interest. I had no doubt the same level of interest would be repeated when I went to Wembley with Spurs, and, sure enough, I was bombarded with telegrams and letters of good wishes. All had the same theme: 'Don't forget Peter, now bring back another winners' medal.'

Thank goodness it worked out that way, or I might have had to spend my summer holiday elsewhere that year. It was the first all-London final and not one which will live in the memory, but Spurs were generally in command and goals by Jimmy Robertson and Frank Saul gave us a 2–0 lead. Even so, the last ten minutes seemed to go on for ever after Bobby Tambling had scored for Chelsea and put them back in the game. I faulted myself a bit for the goal and dreaded the possibility of Chelsea getting an equalizer, but they never really looked like doing it and, after what appeared to be an eternity, the final whistle sounded. I could imagine all Newry sighing with relief.

The celebrations lasted well into the night and the next morning I had my first taste of a victory parade when our open-top bus edged its way through a sea of cheering Spurs fans in Edmonton and Tottenham. It was one of the best occasions in my life.

It's never the same when you have lost at Wembley. Arsenal supporters gave the team a fabulous reception after we'd lost 1–0 to Ipswich in 1978 – but that was a different kind of emotional experience. We knew we hadn't played well and felt a bit like frauds listening to the cheers of fans who must have been as disappointed as we were. It's the ultimate anti-climax. Consolation for the Arsenal lads came a year later when we were able to travel the same route with the Cup as a thank-you gesture for our loyal followers.

Before my move to Highbury, I was to share in two more Spurs successes at Wembley in the League Cup – even if neither quite recaptured the thrill of that FA Cup final victory over Chelsea. Somehow the League Cup never seemed as important and in my first few seasons at White Hart Lane the big clubs – including Spurs – didn't consider it worth entering. That attitude only changed in 1966–67 when it was decided that the final would be staged at Wembley, and the winners would gain entry to the UEFA Cup.

The double lure of cash and a passport to Europe was enough to persuade all 92 League clubs to have a go; yet, ironically, two of the first three finals at Wembley were won by Third Division sides, Queen's Park Rangers and Swindon Town, who were barred from European competition at that time. Even now the early rounds of the League Cup don't compare with the FA Cup, probably because the games are played mid-week and lack the kind of build-up which is inevitable in the FA Cup as Saturday draws nearer.

Spurs had a comfortable passage to the 1971 League Cup Final, being drawn at home in every round and beating Swansea (3–0), Sheffield United (2–1), West Bromwich (5–0) and Coventry (4–1) all at the first attempt. But the going got tougher in the two-leg semi-final against Bristol City. An Alan Gilzean goal gave us a 1–1 draw in the first match at Ashton Gate, and we thought the return a week later at White Hart Lane would be a formality. In fact, the score was 0–0 at the end of 90 minutes and we won 2–0 with Martin Chivers and Jimmy Pearce scoring in extra time. So, once again, we had the benefit of home advantage when we needed it.

There was a gap of more than nine weeks before we went to Wembley and beat Aston Villa, then a Third Division club, 2–0. One of our semi-final matchwinners, Chivers, scored both goals – the other, Pearce, spent the entire game in a track-suit on the bench as substitute.

Centre-half Peter Collins was more fortunate than Jimmy Pearce because he did play at Wembley that year and had an excellent match. Jimmy had to wait another couple of seasons until we beat Norwich City in the 1973 final before he played an active part in winning the League Cup.

When I think about Peter and Jimmy I realize just how lucky I've been during my career, for both were finished by serious injuries at the age of 25 when it seemed to me there was no limit to what they might have achieved.

Peter had been signed from Chelmsford City for a small fee and totalled around 100 first-team games for Spurs, either as deputy for Welsh international Mike England or playing alongside him in the middle of the defence. Peter was as strong as an ox, yet could move like greased lightning for such a big bloke. I always felt comfortable playing behind Peter, and I'm sure he would have developed into one of the outstanding defenders in the First Division but for an ankle injury which forced him out of the game.

Jimmy Pearce, who was most effective operating as a winger but could do a sound job in mid-field or anywhere in attack, was loaded with talent and most of the other Spurs players expected him eventually to win an England cap. We all appreciated his worth to the team, even though he didn't always get the credit he deserved from the fans.

Jimmy was a Tottenham boy who had graduated from the junior ranks at a time when Spurs tended to splash out in the transfer market for a big name if they needed a striker. He had a constant battle to hold a regular first-team place and, considering he was in and out of the side, did well to make more than 100 First Division appearances before a persistently troublesome knee made him quit. He had superb ball control and a powerful shot in either foot. On a day when Chivers, Gilzean and Pearce were all on song, Spurs took some stopping – and I was delighted that one of his last games for the club was in a Wembley final.

That 1973 final against Norwich produced another example of fluctuating fortunes, involving two players, and proved yet again that you can never be certain what fate has in store. John Pratt and Ralph Coates were alike in the sense that both would cover every blade of grass and run until they dropped, even if inclined to be a trifle unpredictable in their use of the ball. Perhaps it was because they were similar in style that there was only room for one in the team to play Norwich.

Pratt, a product of the club's youth scheme, was chosen, a deserved reward for the stalwart service he gave Spurs both before and after that Cup final. Coates, a big money buy from Burnley, was named as substitute and was understandably disappointed. But John's dream-come-true turned into a nightmare when he was injured early in a game which was to mark his only Wembley appearance, and Ralph came on to replace him in the 25th minute.

I still have a mental picture of Pratt taking his long, slow walk to the dressing room and I'm sure he was near to tears. Spurs finished 1–0 winners and, in true story-book fashion, it was Coates who scored the deciding goal – making history as the first sub to emerge as a match-winner in a League Cup final.

It was a pretty ordinary game, but since Spurs played in 23 cup-ties that season I think we can claim that we earned some kind of reward. We had taken nine games to get to Wembley, needing three matches and extra time to beat Middlesbrough in the third round and another dose of extra time before overcoming Wolves in the semi-finals.

We had three FA Cup-ties and ten games in the UEFA Cup. It was ironic that we eventually went out of Europe against English opposition when, in the semi-finals, Liverpool beat us on the away-goals rule. That was revenge for Liverpool, one of our victims – in a White Hart Lane replay – in the League Cup. Since we also met them twice in the First Division I can honestly say Spurs and Liverpool were sick of the sight of each other by the season's end.

There wasn't much Cup excitement in my last four seasons with Spurs, but things changed with a vengeance when I moved to Arsenal and figured in FA Cup finals in each of my first three seasons at Highbury. Wembley was on the horizon right from the start when Arsenal went to Bramall Lane in a third-round match in January 1978 and won 5–0. We couldn't put a foot wrong that afternoon, and I even saved a penalty.

We didn't need a single replay that year, beating Wolves (2–1), Walsall (4–1) and Wrexham (3–2) on the way to a London semi-final against Orient at Stamford Bridge. Arsenal were odds-on to win that match and, despite the obvious pitfalls of overconfidence when you play a side from a lower division, the feeling in the dressing room was that we ought to do it with a couple of goals to spare.

In the event, Arsenal had all the luck that was going as we beat Orient 3–0. Our first two goals came when Orient defenders deflected shots from Malcolm Macdonald past keeper John Jackson. On each occasion the ball could have flown in any direction – but it was our day, so it flew into the net.

Arsenal started hot favourites at Wembley to defeat Ipswich Town, playing in their first-ever Cup final and admitting to being worried before the kick-off by injuries to Kevin Beattie and Allan Hunter. But Ipswich upset the form-book by winning 1–0 and it could easily have been 3–0.

It was a well kept secret before the game that we had our injury problems at Highbury as well, with Pat Rice, Sammy Nelson and Liam Brady all striving to pass fitness tests. Brady didn't last out the 90 minutes and was replaced by substitute Graham Rix, while it wasn't until a couple of weeks later that close scrutiny of an X-ray revealed Nelson had played at Wembley with cracked ribs.

I record these facts as some kind of explanation, not as an excuse. Ipswich thoroughly deserved to win – John Wark hit the post twice – and Arsenal simply weren't at the races that afternoon.

Apart from that little World Cup defeat by England 15 years earlier, it was my first losing Cup final at Wembley. I'd had a reasonably good match but that was scant consolation as I sat afterwards in a dressing room which resembled a morgue. Several of the Arsenal players cried unashamedly, and we all felt humiliated.

A great deal of criticism was heaped on the Arsenal players for our inept performance, but one whom I felt should have been exempted was Alan Hudson – easily our best player. It was a shame that Alan left Highbury the following season, for he had so much to offer. Often I would stand in goal and marvel at his talent, seeing the obvious frustration of opponents who couldn't get near him.

It has been said that Alan's attitude was suspect, and it's true enough that he didn't conform any more than George Best. Not every player can have the temperament of Bobby Charlton, but when it came to training Hudson was beyond reproach. He was always ready to continue with his exercises and body-work after all the other Arsenal players had showered and left for home. Alan should have had a cupboard full of England caps and, although I don't doubt he enjoyed himself playing in the United States with Seattle Sounders after leaving Arsenal, his departure was a sad loss for English football.

When Arsenal returned to Wembley the season after the Ipswich defeat, and came close to another disaster against Manchester United, the team showed two changes. Hudson had gone and injury had prematurely ended the scoring exploits of Malcolm Macdonald. The gaps were filled by Rix and Brian Talbot, signed from Ipswich after helping to beat us a year earlier.

Talbot's successive Wembley wins with different clubs was unique, yet he must have wondered if he'd even get a Cup game with Arsenal that season. When he arrived we were in the middle of a remarkable third-round serial with Sheffield Wednesday. We needed five games and nine hours' football to get past the Third Division club, and might well have been out of the FA Cup before Talbot's transfer was completed after the second of those matches.

The first meeting, on a snow-covered pitch at Hillsborough, ended in a 1–1 draw which was a fair reflection of the play – so we went into the Highbury replay in naturally optimistic mood. But Wednesday gave us a chasing that night and led 1–0 until the 90th minute. One of their players actually remarked to David O'Leary, 'sorry to beat you, but we can do with the bonus', as the time ticked away. Then, right out of the blue, Liam Brady equalized following a corner-kick and Arsenal were reprieved. In fact, we were all so relieved that it didn't matter too much when the game ended level at 1–1 after extra time.

With Brian Talbot sitting in the stand, no doubt biting his nails, we had three more matches with Wednesday – all at Filbert Street, Leicester – before finally winning 2–0 with goals from Frank Stapleton and Steve Gatting. It was another of those personal hard-luck stories that Gatting, having scored a vital goal to help break the deadlock, was replaced by Talbot for the next round at home to Notts County. And Brian celebrated by hitting the target in a 2–0 victory.

When Arsenal were drawn to visit Nottingham Forest, who were unbeaten at home, not many people fancied our chances. But against the odds, and the run of play, we won 1–0 with a tremendous Frank Stapleton header. It was one of those nights for me, and I rate it among my best Cup displays. At the final whistle you had to feel sorry for Forest, who played so well without getting the breaks.

Southampton was the next stop. We drew 1–1 and took the replay 2–0 to qualify for a Villa Park semi-final with Wolves. But the win over Southampton wasn't achieved without cost, for Brady aggravated a knee injury and had to be replaced by Steve Walford. Liam left Highbury limping heavily and with only ten days to go before the semi-final it was clear he wouldn't make it.

Liam had intensive treatment in a forlorn hope that he might be OK, but he refused to take a gamble and risk letting the team down in such an important match. He wasn't bothered by any personal consideration, but by the memory of what had happened at Wembley the previous May when he'd taken a chance and failed to last the distance.

It is always a debatable point whether or not a star player should go into action when obviously less than fully fit, yet if you always waited until you were a hundred per cent you'd miss half of the games some seasons. With such a crowded programme it's inevitable that players are often carrying knocks from the previous match. Usually the public are unaware of the fact.

I've frequently heard a manager or a coach telling a player with a painful knee or a sore ankle, 'You'll be all right, son, don't worry about it.' Sometimes they change their viewpoint afterwards – a lot depends upon the result.

Fortunately, we managed comfortably enough without Liam. Back came Steve Gatting to do a sound job and we beat Wolves 2–0 with Frank Stapleton and Alan Sunderland sharing the goals.

So it was Wembley once again, with the pressure eased because our opponents were Manchester United and a slight shade of odds favoured them to win. It was a nice change to be regarded as the underdogs, something I'd not previously experienced in a Cup final. The rest of the lads relished it as well.

Arsenal turned on the style in the first half with goals from Talbot and Stapleton. United did not give us as many problems as we'd expected, and our defence dealt with the threatening Joe Jordan – and Gordon McQueen when he came upfield for free-kicks and corners – without too much sweat.

The score was still the same with four minutes to go and we were getting ready to go up the steps to collect the Cup when United caught us with the old one-two. Suddenly it was 2–2 and all hell seemed to be breaking loose. Visions of the Sunday morning headlines loomed before my eyes. I could see 'Arsenal Collapse' in huge black type.

The prospect of extra time was anything but appealing now that the advantage had passed to United. Maybe they got caught up in their own euphoria at coming back from the dead – whatever the reason, Arsenal launched a telling counter-attack from a magnificent Brady pass, Rix crossed from the left while running at full speed and Sunderland raced to the far post to slam in the winner. It was a Cup final which will be talked about for many years to come.

Nobody was more pleased than Terry Neill and Don Howe, who had made a surprise substitution by sending on Steve Walford for David Price when it seemed the game was locked up at 2–0. My feeling was that it wasn't so much a tactical switch, but a gesture to Steve for his contribution in earlier rounds. It was a commendable thought and a move which would have gone unnoticed had the score remained the same. Yet while our late lapse certainly wasn't Steve's fault, you can guess what would have been said and written with hindsight had United won. Terry and Don must have been the two luckiest fellows in the world when Alan Sunderland provided the happy ending.

The pendulum was to swing again the following year when Arsenal lost 1–0 to West Ham at Wembley. It was hinted that we underestimated West Ham because they were a Second Division side, yet nothing could be further from the truth. They had too many talented individuals to be taken lightly, and a shrewd manager–coach partnership in John Lyall and my old pal Eddie Baily.

If Arsenal were below our best that day I can only suggest that we were suffering from fixture-lag because we were also heavily involved in Europe and the First Division. The squad wasn't strong enough to cope with so many games in such a short space of time. We had been fully extended in a semi-final with Liverpool that went to four matches before we eventually beat them at Coventry just 12 days prior to Wembley. It reduced the time usually available for preparation for a Cup final. But all credit to West Ham – that night London really belonged to them.

11

FUN AND GAMES ABROAD

Soon after I came to England in 1963 the football world was rocked by the 'Bribes Scandal' which resulted in several players being banned and subsequently sent to prison. It was a terrible shock to most people connected with the game, who assumed that such things only went on in places like Italy or South America. British Soccer had always been above suspicion.

I remember being appalled that any footballer could be foolish enough to ruin his career for a couple of hundred pounds – but I never felt it was up to me to sit in judgment, since I didn't know the circumstances which prompted the players involved to succumb to temptation. All I can record after 19 years in the game is that I've never been approached to give away a goal or fix a match. You hear rumours from time to time, but almost without exception they are totally untrue.

There was, however, one occasion when I was with Spurs that the entire team had a bet on a match – and it paid off. It happened when we were touring in a certain African country. Just before our final game we were told by the chairman of the local club who had arranged the tour that there was a bill of £400 outstanding for the drinks we had ordered with our meals. Spurs were refusing to pay it.

We hadn't been hitting the bottle. The players had been relaxing on an end-of-season trip and divided between about 18 of us, spread over a couple of weeks, it wasn't an outrageous sum. But the Spurs directors said it wasn't the responsibility of the club, and we would have to cough up.

Alan Gilzean, who liked a drink, was so incensed at what he regarded as the mean attitude of the directors that he was ready to sign a personal cheque on the spot – but the rest of the lads insisted that the bill must be split equally between us. We knew the tour sponsors couldn't afford it, and the last thing we wanted was to give our hosts the impression that the Spurs players were free-loaders. Our personal reputations, quite apart from the good name of the club, were at stake.

That was when our African friend suddenly came up with a bright idea. He pointed out that local bookmakers were offering odds against the correct score of our final match, and if we could win by a certain margin we could raise the cash to pay our debt.

We held an impromptu team meeting and decided that 6–0 was about right. The odds were 10–1, so we had a whip-round and duly invested £40 to win us £400.

I won't forget that game in a hurry. I felt I was under more pressure than any of the other players, knowing that if I let in a goal our bet would be a loser. Luckily, I wasn't overworked and managed a clean sheet while the lads went about their business at the other end.

It wasn't easy, for the home goalkeeper had an inspired match and pulled off a series of spectacular saves. Even when Spurs went 5–0 up he was diving all over the place, turning shots round the posts and over the bar. There was no more than 90 seconds left when we scored our sixth goal among scenes of jubilation that must have convinced the crowd the sun had got at us.

All the Tottenham players learned a lesson that day – that it's not simple to score goals against any opposition. We really had to sweat for our money.

There was a great deal of resentment against the Spurs directors for putting us in such a position. No doubt they felt the players were out of order in signing for drinks with meals, yet I can't believe any other First Division club would have made such a big issue of it.

I certainly noticed the difference when I was loaned to Stoke City for a trip to the Far East. I don't think I've ever been on such a happy tour. Instead of the division between 'them' and 'us' which existed with Spurs, the Stoke directors mixed with the players on equal terms and were always first at the bar. The season was over, everybody was relaxed and Stoke chairman, the late Albert Henshall, and his fellow directors treated the players like men instead of little boys.

Stoke had a goalkeeper problem because first-choice Peter Shilton had other commitments before the tour was arranged and wasn't available for the full trip. Gordon Banks was on the coaching staff at the time but, after his eye injury, there was a doubt whether he would be able to play – and Stoke had promised to field a full-strength team.

It was Morris Keston, the well known Spurs fan and a close friend of the Stoke manager Tony Waddington and his board, who suggested I might be willing to travel. Tony got permission from Tottenham and I agreed because I'd never visited Indonesia where most of the matches were being played.

I never regretted it. Although there were plenty of travel problems – I think we missed every connecting flight – it was a bundle of laughs all the way. And Tony and all the Stoke players made me feel as though I'd been with the club for years.

There was almost an unfunny finish to the trip when we flew to Singapore for the last night before returning to England. I was one of several players who were nearly kept behind by the local authorities.

When we arrived in Singapore and were passing through Passport Control, five or six of us were told to stand to one side. We had no idea what was going on until a young lady turned up and said she was taking us all to have our hair cut.

Long hair was the fashion in Britain at the time, but it wasn't acceptable in Singapore and we had been singled out to prove the point. We were frantic. A messenger was sent to get Tony Waddington, who had to use all his powers of persuasion before a compromise was reached. We were told our passports would be impounded, and they would be returned next morning for the flight to England only if we had our locks trimmed when we reached the team hotel.

It was a temporary reprieve, but in common with the other lads I had no intention of allowing a Singapore Sweeney Todd to hack off my hair. The thought of returning home looking like an escaped convict was too much to stomach.

So, amidst a non-stop flow of wisecracks from the rest of the players who were naturally enjoying the joke, we tried to take evasive action the following morning before setting out to the airport. We flattened our hair with water and even used small hair-grips to attempt to give the impression we had shortened it. But it was a windy day, the hair quickly dried out and it was soon spilling over our collars.

The joke was now on us, for a high-ranking airport official, who was anything but amused, declared that if we didn't have our hair cut we would be kept behind while the rest of the party left for home. It needed more diplomacy from manager Waddington before our passports were flung at us with the solemn warning: 'Don't come back to Singapore.' It was touch and go, for our plane was warming up and the passenger steps were about to be wheeled away as we dashed across the tarmac to board.

I have never been so glad to get out of a foreign city. But I wouldn't mind returning to Indonesia. Despite obvious signs of poverty, the fans there gave Stoke a wonderful reception with crowds of 60,000 at the matches cheering every move. A lot of the credit for engendering such goodwill belonged to the Stoke directors, for it was a rule that every player in the party – even those not taking part in a game – should get changed and take part in the pre-match warm-up. The fans were just as enthusiastic about the shooting-in and ball-skill exhibitions as they were about the match itself.

While I've made my point that players object to being treated like little boys, I have to admit that they sometimes get up to some childish pranks in the relaxing atmosphere of a foreign tour. I recall one Spurs defender who, in France, went into a local shoe shop and had the place in uproar because he insisted he wanted to buy only one slipper instead of the customary pair. He maintained that since he only kicked with one foot he wore a slipper on the other one. By the time he left, shaking his head because his request had been turned down, the shop assistants were totally convinced the English must be stark, raving bonkers.

There was another occasion in Malaga, on Spain's Costa del Sol, when the fun and games got a bit hectic when the Spurs players were all sitting around the hotel pool after a match. One or two of the lads were throwing everything they could lay their hands upon into the pool – you had to be quick or your sun-glasses or sun oil would suddenly disappear with a splash.

Our centre-half Maurice Norman had left his shirt on the back of his chair, and even that didn't escape. It went into the pool and floated on the top of the water. That didn't satisfy Cyril Knowles, who took a running jump and landed on top of the shirt to submerge it completely. A split second later Cyril's outstretched arm was clutching the camera he forgot he had tied round his wrist. Cyril's face was a picture when he climbed out and discovered all his film had been ruined. It gave the rest of us a laugh and cured Cyril for all time.

Another gag which misfired, and nearly had far more serious consequences, came at the end of a Spurs trip to Mauritius. We had enjoyed ourselves and struck up a particularly friendly relationship with the waiters at the hotel. They were always smiling and ready to join in our jokes. Nothing was too much trouble for them and the players willingly clubbed together for a thank-you tip.

Just before we left for the airport we were sitting round the pool when one of the waiters came to say goodbye. He was promptly chucked in the deep end. As he disappeared one of his pals came rushing up and shouted that he couldn't swim – so full-back Terry Naylor, who had pushed him in, dived in fully clothed to rescue the poor fellow.

It all happened in the matter of a split second, and the soaked waiter had fortunately come to no harm – perhaps he thought we had every intention of pulling him out at the time. Terry was more shaken, and undoubtedly more uncomfortable when he had to travel to the airport in wet gear because all his other stuff had already gone on ahead.

Having travelled to most parts of the soccer-playing world, I have often been asked which stadium I regard as the most impressive. It's a difficult question to answer. Wembley and Glasgow's Hampden Park both take some beating for atmosphere, and Windsor Park, Belfast, has a special place in my affections. Yet not even patriotism could place them at the top of the list.

I've been told by other players that the Maracana Stadium in Rio de Janiero is in a class of its own. It holds 200,000 and I can imagine it must be something special when Brazil are playing there in an important international match. But since I've never been to Rio I'll have to take their word for it.

The finest I've seen is the Aztec Stadium in Mexico City, which has a capacity of more than 100,000 and is really a sight to behold when it is packed. I remember it particularly well, for I played there – for Spurs against the Mexican national side – on my 21st birthday in June 1966.

That game was billed as a warm-up for Mexico before they left for England to take part in the 1966 World Cup, and believe me they weren't kidding. The kick-off was at noon and I've never been so hot in my life. I felt absolutely scorched by the time the final whistle went – and I wasn't running about. Remarkably, in the conditions, Spurs won 1–0 and Keith Weller had a fantastic match.

Israel is another hot spot, but conditions haven't been too bad on the three occasions I've played there for Northern Ireland – once in Jaffa and twice in Tel-aviv. I had a particularly good game when Ireland drew 0–0 in the first of our qualifying ties for the 1982 World Cup, but it was my previous visit in March 1976 which sticks in the memory for a different reason.

I travelled a day after the rest of the team because I stayed back to go to London's Hilton Hotel to collect the Professional Footballers' Association statuette as Player of the Year. When I boarded the plane for Tel-aviv at Heathrow the next morning I received a bonus, for the pilot invited me up front into the first-class compartment.

That wasn't the end of it. The Israeli Football Association generously gave me another award on arrival after hearing I'd got the PFA statuette, and the Irish lads also had a collection for me. It's typical of the team spirit in the Northern Ireland camp, for the players must have thought they were always having to dig into their pockets: they made other presentations when I won my 50th cap and again when I broke the record for international appearances.

It is a fabulous feeling to be chosen by your peers as number one, and I certainly wasn't expecting the PFA honour. Spurs were going through a pretty ordinary patch and, while I was happy with my form, I had no reason to think I would top the poll. In fact, when I learned I was among the top six contenders I was pleased, but thought little more of it. It did cross my mind that I had been included in the best-of-the-season First Division eleven. But that was all.

Even on the night I didn't think I had won. The PFA officials had simply told me that they wanted all six candidates to be present. Since Northern Ireland didn't mind me flying to Israel 24 hours later, I had no objections.

When I arrived at the Hilton I spotted Kevin Keegan, who I felt was favourite, shaking hands with PFA secretary Cliff Lloyd. I thought Kevin was being congratulated for winning the award, which just shows how you can jump to a wrong conclusion. In the end Kevin had to wait until 1982 to collect.

I got quite a surprise when the envelope was opened and my name was read out. I made my way to the microphone to say a few words of thanks and that was the biggest ordeal, for I'm not too hot when it comes to making a speech.

I've had my fair share of awards, for I was elected as Spurs Player of the Year on four occasions and in 1973 I won the Football Writers' Association trophy as Footballer of the Year. That gave me as much pleasure as the players' award, except that I was told a couple of weeks in advance and worried so much about having to make a speech that I didn't really enjoy my meal. Fortunately, it all went off well.

I was only the second Spurs player to get the prize, Danny Blanchflower having previously won it twice – and he was a Northern Irishman as well. I feel Spurs' success in winning the League Cup that season was a big boost, plus the fact that I had received a great deal of publicity about that time I saved two Liverpool penalty-kicks at Anfield.

There is always a special drama associated with a penalty, with the spotlight on both the player taking the kick and the goalkeeper facing it. It's a wonderful feeling to make a save from the spot, even if it's often a case of being lucky and choosing the right direction to move. But, since the odds are invariably loaded against a goalkeeper, I'd be quite happy to go a season without having to face a single penalty.

I'm glad that I've only been involved once in a penalty shoot-out to decide an important game. On that occasion, I finished on the losing side when Arsenal met Spanish club Valencia in the European Cup-winners' Cup final in Brussels in May 1980.

We had beaten Italy's Juventus in the semi-finals, thanks to a late goal by young Paul Vaessen in Turin, and fancied our chances of following up with a win over Valencia. We should have done so, for, although I made a couple of good saves, Arsenal had most of the scoring opportunities. But the Spanish goalkeeper was right on song and the game ended 0–0 after extra time.

I'm sure the players on both sides would have preferred a replay, for that must be the most satisfactory way to settle a vital match, but the rules had changed since Chelsea had won the same trophy with a replay victory over Real Madrid in Athens in 1971. In Brussels we had to go through the penalty ritual, which I suppose was better than tossing a coin.

It looked good for Arsenal when I made a save from Valencia's star player, Argentinian striker Mario Kempes. I'd seen TV clips of Kempes taking a penalty and, as he ran up, I thought 'If he puts this one where I think he will, I can get to it'. Kempes obliged, I dived to my right and reached the ball. I must admit it wasn't a very good penalty.

Unfortunately, it was my one and only save and, when Liam Brady and Graham Rix both failed, Valencia won the shoot-out 6–5. It was a bit hard to take, particularly as we felt that the referee was slack in allowing the Valencia keeper to move early on almost every kick. He was well on his way when he stopped the decider from Rix.

My one consolation is that I was spared the ordeal of taking a penalty, which would have been necessary if the score had remained level after all the other lads had had a go. I don't think I lack confidence, yet I wouldn't have fancied it.

I remember the 1974 FA Charity Shield between Liverpool and Leeds at Wembley, which was also decided by penalties. Liverpool collected the Shield after Leeds goalkeeper David Harvey had shot over the bar. It provided a false result and the FA obviously thought so, for they changed the rules and now the Shield is held by each club for six months in the event of a draw after 90 minutes. The Football League, on the other hand, now decree that a penalty shoot-out must take place if the League Cup final ends with the scores level after extra time in a replay. So far, thank goodness, it hasn't been necessary.

I have never forgotten how upset both Brady and Rix felt after that Cup-winners' final in Brussels, but there were no recriminations from the rest of the Arsenal players. We all knew it could have happened to anybody.

It may sound all right in theory to claim that a professional footballer should never miss a penalty, but it doesn't work out like that in practice. Even the most accurate of penalty takers, like Glenn Hoddle of Spurs, fail sometimes.

There's no magic formula – a player can blast the ball or try to place it. If he relies on power there is a chance he will hit the goalkeeper or miss the target altogether. If he goes for accuracy there's bound to be a day when his calculations are a few inches adrift. The margin between success and failure can be that slender.

That defeat by Valencia came in my third European final, but the previous two – when I was with Spurs – were in the UEFA Cup and decided over two legs.

When Spurs won the trophy in 1972 it was something of an anti-climax because our opponents in the final were Wolves and, although the prize at stake was important, it seemed unnatural to be playing against another English club. The atmosphere usually connected with the event was missing – and it felt odd to be at 'home', so to speak, in both games after journeys to Iceland, France, Rumania (twice) and Italy in previous rounds. We won the first match at Molyneux 2–1, and only needed to draw the return at White Hart Lane. That's exactly what we did, for the result was 1–1.

There was a similar situation the following season when Spurs were knocked out of the UEFA Cup by Liverpool in the semi-finals, losing on the away-goals rule when defeated 1–0 at Anfield and then winning the second leg 2–1 at White Hart Lane. Liverpool did at least keep the trophy in England, and everybody at Spurs thought we were going to get it back the next year.

The 1974 campaign began with a flattering 5–1 victory over Zurich Grasshoppers in Switzerland, and from that point we seemed to go from strength to strength. Spurs never lost a match as we sailed through to the final.

We polished off Grasshoppers with a 4–1 win, to make it 9–2 on aggregate, and then soundly beat Aberdeen 4–1 at White Hart Lane after a 1–1 draw at Pittodrie Park. Dynamo Tbilisi, of Russia, gave us a hard time on their ground and we were happy to come away with a 1–1 draw. Manager Bill Nicholson warned us it would be just as tough at home, but we outplayed Dinamo and romped to a 5–1 win. Now our confidence was sky-high and we defeated Cologne 2–1 in West Germany and 3–0 at home, and then accounted for the East Germans of Lokomotive Leipzig by 2–1 and 2–0 in the semi-finals.

Maybe we counted our chickens too soon, for Spurs came sadly unstuck in the final. When we met Feyenoord of Holland our forwards, who had been piling up the goals in earlier matches, couldn't hit the target. We drew the first match at Tottenham 2–2 with centre-half Mike England scoring our opener and a Dutch defender, van Daele, putting the ball through his own goal, and then we lost the second leg 2–0 in Rotterdam.

It was a bad night for the club in every respect, for Spurs' fans went on the rampage, tearing out seats and hurling them on to the pitch. I don't know exactly what sparked off their behaviour – although it was quite obvious that some had had too much to drink – but it blackened Spurs' previous good reputation on the continent.

UEFA responded with a five-year ban on Spurs: if the club qualified for Europe again during that period the first two home matches would have to be played a distance of 200 miles from London. The ruling was never enforced because it was to be another eight seasons – by which time I had moved to Arsenal – before Spurs were to win a European place and take part in the Cup-winners' Cup.

The irony of the situation is that I recall the wonderful reception the Spurs players got from our supporters when we walked out to inspect the pitch before the game in Rotterdam. They were singing and appeared to be not only well behaved, but also in the mood to enjoy the game.

Bill Nicholson looked up at the sea of blue and white and said, 'Just listen to them, aren't they fantastic? You have got to go out and win for them.' He was obviously proud that so many fans had made the trip.

Bill's pride changed to disgust after the riot began. He was asked by UEFA officials to broadcast an appeal over the loudspeakers at half-time for the Spurs contingent to cool down. He came back into the dressing room, his face as black as thunder, calling the fans some quite unrepeatable names. His change of attitude from an hour or so earlier would have been funny had it not been so tragic.

The pity was, as always happens in such a situation, that it ruined the occasion for the majority of innocent Spurs supporters. When they tried to leave the ground before the end of the game, some of them were belted by Dutch police who had lost their patience and were apparently hitting out at anybody wearing a Spurs scarf.

Not that the disturbance influenced the result. Although the players were aware of the trouble, the pitch at the Feyenoord Stadium is so far removed from the crowd that it would be ridiculous for me to pretend that it affected our performance. We got what we deserved over the 90 minutes – nothing.

12

GEORGE BEST

George Best built two reputations during his footballing career, one for his skill on the field and the other for his exploits off it. I don't know about a split personality, but it seems that George was two different fellows – and I have to admit that I only knew one of them.

As a player, Best was quite simply the finest I ever saw. I never came up against Pelé, who is generally acknowledged to be the greatest of them all. But if it's true he was better than George then he must have come from another planet.

Like everybody else, I have read all the stories about George's sex life and his drinking bouts and even now I find it difficult to believe most of them. Obviously some of them are true as George has rushed into print on several occasions to tell the world how he jumped in and out of bed and propped up countless bars, though I have a sneaking feeling he was guilty of a bit of blarney at times. It just doesn't sound like my pal George, my room-mate on every occasion we were both picked for Northern Ireland.

We first met back in April 1964, when we both made our international débuts against Wales at Vetch Field, Swansea. I was 18 – George was a year younger – and a Third Division player with Watford when I got that first cap. My selection came out of the blue, for I certainly wasn't expecting to be picked in preference to Harry Gregg, but the Irish had taken an 8–3 Wembley hammering from England in the previous match and the selectors had decided to make a few changes.

Football at international level was something new to me. It was the era before substitutes, and I hadn't been included previously in an Irish squad since the custom was to call up just one goalkeeper. When I reported to the team headquarters, it was a relief to learn that George had also been picked – to replace Billy Bingham at outside-right – and that I wasn't the 'baby' of the party.

I'd never met George before: in fact I had only heard of him in a vague fashion as a lad who'd played a few First Division matches on the right wing for Manchester United. I assumed he couldn't be a mug because United at that time were loaded with talented forwards such as Bobby Charlton and Denis Law, but I had no idea just how good he was, and didn't have a hint of how great he was going to become.

Because we were both so young we were paired off as room-mates, two new boys full of ambition. We struck up a friendship from the off which was continued throughout the years ahead. My first impression of him was as a quiet lad, and neither of us had much to say. We spent the couple of days before the match mainly training or sleeping.

We beat the Welsh 3–2 and I had an ordinary sort of game, nothing brilliant but no mistakes. George did well, although he didn't score. He looked decidedly useful for his size.

A fortnight later exactly the same Northern Ireland team was selected against Uruguay in Belfast and we won 3–0. It was a good match for both George and myself: not exactly outstanding, but enough to raise hopes we would become regulars in the line-up.

Everybody was beginning to sense George's potential, yet he was hardly in the superstar class at that stage. Nearly two years were to elapse before he jumped into that bracket after hitting the headlines with a fantastic performance when Manchester United defeated Benfica 5–1 in a European Cup quarter-final in Lisbon. That was the turning point when Best, with his dark, good looks and modern hair-style, was dubbed 'El Beatle' by the popular press.

He didn't change then and he never altered in all the years we shared a room. That may be hard to swallow, but I always found him basically the same quiet lad I met at Swansea. If George didn't change, the attitude of people towards him did in a very big way. Talk about instant fame – the transformation was incredible.

All George wanted was to be one of the boys, to have a drink and a chat with the rest of the team. Like me, he liked nothing better than to sit and listen to the old-timers talking about previous international games. Two or three lagers was his intake, no more and no less than most of the other players.

That was the usual pattern in the first two years of his international career, and when we played in Belfast both George and I would go out shopping the day before a game with no more than the odd greeting from passers-by.

Then it all began to happen. George was besieged by well-wishers the moment he put a foot outside the team hotel, pestered for auto-graphs at every turn. That soon put an end to the shopping expeditions. Inside the hotels, which were open to the public, quite apart from the girls who were trying to catch his eye, fans used to surround George in the bar to talk about the match or about Manchester United.

It wasn't just in Britain. When we played abroad, on either side of the Iron Curtain, it was just like the pop-scene with Best the non-stop focus of attention. It didn't make him big-headed. What it did do was make his life a misery.

Wherever we went it was the same – hundreds of fans outside the hotel chanting 'We want George, we want George.' We found we couldn't even have a sleep on the afternoon before a match because of the din.

The very high expectations of the fans began to worry George. He wasn't the type to get hot and bothered before the kick-off, for he would sit in the corner of the dressing room reading the programme totally relaxed while the rest of us were all wound up. It was as though George was going out to play in a practice match instead of an international in front of a vast crowd. But he confessed to me that he sensed the fans were expecting too much, disappointed when he didn't run half the length of the field beating three or four opponents at a time. And he felt that when he didn't deliver the goods he was letting them down.

I've never been subjected to off-field pressures on the Best scale, but I do have some idea of what it is like when you are put on a pedestal as a player. After I won the Footballer of the Year award in 1973 I began to feel conscious of the burden of living up to my reputation. Each time I played, especially in away matches, I realized I was under great scrutiny from the fans and that even the slightest mistake would provoke criticism. If I failed to catch a ball cleanly, I could imagine the buzz going round the terraces: 'How did he ever become Footballer of the Year?'

It was after four or five years of this kind of treatment that George began to go off the rails, turning up late for training with Manchester United and sometimes not even putting in an appearance. In the early seventies he would go missing for days at a time.

George needed to be at the top all the time, and I felt he found it hard to take when things were not going well. He accepted that Northern Ireland could never be the best, and maybe he took it badly when Manchester United began to slip – he wanted to be in Europe every season.

It was when United started to wane that they began to have problems with George. The slump might have started a season or two earlier but for his efforts and it was accentuated when George put his lifestyle before his football commitment and somehow lost his way.

When I heard the reports that George was drinking heavily, I was mystified. I can honestly say I'd never regarded him as a serious drinker: there was no drinking on the sly in our hotel room, and George had never shown any craving for a drink in my company. Only once when we were together with Northern Ireland do I remember him having a few too many, and that was after a game. We both got stuck into the brandy that night, which ended in our hotel room with me placing newspapers on the floor and challenging George to walk a straight line. He could, too, but only just.

George's bad timekeeping spread to international matches. He would report late for pre-match get-togethers, sometimes by a matter of hours and occasionally the day after the team. A succession of Irish managers had a dreadful time trying to impose some form of discipline on George on the basis that he was no different to the rest of us. Yet we all knew he *was* different. Because of the strain he was under, none of the other Irish lads ever resented the way George carried on. We were only too pleased to see him when he did turn up, regardless of how late. Because he never put on any airs and graces with us, George was always welcome.

We all knew he was more than a bit special, and that Northern Ireland's chances of winning any particular game probably depended upon whether or not George was in the team. He stood out in any company and, with Irish resources so limited, George was even more valuable to us. Eventually the team officials came to live with George's bad timekeeping, conscious that he was worth an extra 10,000 on the gate.

Northern Ireland have never had a player remotely as good as Best in my time. About the only one ever to be mentioned in the same breath as George was Peter Doherty – an inside-forward who starred just before and immediately after the war and later became manager of the national side.

Doherty was in charge during the great purple patch in Northern Ireland's history when the team qualified for the 1958 World Cup in Sweden and lasted longer in the competition than either England or Scotland. I have heard Danny Blanchflower talking about Doherty's skill as a player, and he must have been tremendous. But if Peter was the George Best of his era on the field, it was in the days before so much fuss was made about footballers – by the media in general and television in particular – and he could enjoy the quiet life off the field.

Thinking back, I can't recall anybody hanging around the team hotel in my first couple of years with Ireland. We could have been a group of businessmen attending the firm's conference for all the attention we attracted. That all changed completely after George became something of a national personality.

It used to bother me that all the fuss surrounding George wherever he went would put him off playing in international matches. That is why I would always have my fingers crossed until I saw him appear. When he did appear, my spirits would rise because I felt Northern Ireland could win any game when George was playing.

That feeling never altered. When George was named in the initial squad for a vital World Cup qualifying match against Scotland in Belfast in 1981 – a game which, at the time, we thought we needed to win in order to qualify for Spain – I was absolutely delighted. George had been playing in America with San Jose Earthquakes and, at 35, I know the critics argued he wasn't capable of lasting 90 minutes in a vital World Cup game. I suppose they were right, but I believed he could do enough if he played for half the match or came on as substitute if we needed him.

I backed Billy Bingham's gamble in putting Best in the squad of 22 all the way. But, as events turned out, George struggled when San Jose played in Britain during a short tour the week before the Scotland game. Both he and manager Bingham accepted that the great comeback wasn't possible. There was a feeling of intense disappointment in the camp when he failed to make it: we all remembered the past.

I have said George didn't cause us any problems, but that isn't strictly accurate. In training sessions he would be a problem because nobody could ever get the ball off him in five-a-side games. He could keep it as long as he liked, indulging in the footballer's favourite ploy of 'nutmegging' opponents – the trade description for putting the ball through the legs of a challenger.

George was in a class of his own. Even when one-touch rules were applied in those training games, it made little difference. George would just knock the ball against the legs of his opponents and collect the rebound.

When George was at his peak, he had the lot. He had electrifying pace; he could shoot with either foot; he was good in the air considering his size; and his tackling was unbelievable. He also had stamina, and people forget the terrific effort he put into every game. In the early days he would sometimes lose the ball in the other penalty area, then chase all the way back to our own 'box' to retrieve it. This is what was so special about him. So many other wingers of that era had plenty of skill, but when they lost the ball they waited for a team-mate to get it back. Not George. He'd come flying back, win the ball and then set off upfield on yet another run. He was perpetual motion personified.

Those who refer to George as a 'flashy' player don't do him justice. He was an all-rounder, and his commitment made him the nearest I've seen to a perfect footballer. There was just nobody to touch him.

George made only 38 appearances for Northern Ireland – a tragic waste of his talents when you realize he should have at least doubled that total and challenged me for a record number of caps. Probably his peak performance was in a 1–0 victory over Scotland in Belfast.

Nobody could get the ball off him in that match, and by the end I noticed that several famous Scottish players had stopped even trying to do so. It seemed they wanted to be anywhere on the field except where Best was doing his stuff. I honestly didn't blame them: when you met George on a day like that he gave you an inferiority complex.

Many years later, in a World Cup qualifier in Holland in 1977, George turned in another fantastic display. He outshone everybody else on the field to earn Northern Ireland a 2–2 draw against a team then reckoned the top in Europe – a team which went on to reach the 1978 World Cup final and only lost to hosts Argentina in extra time. The Dutch fans gave George a marvellous ovation that night and he earned it.

The Dutch detailed Johann Neeskens to mark George in that match. Neeskens was some player, but George made a monkey out of him and 'nut-megged' the Dutch star so often that he finished by offering Neeskens a tie-up from his socks to tie his legs together. Arrogant? Of course, but it was a gesture which indicated that George knew he was having a magical game.

Perhaps the memory of games like that kidded me that George could still have done his stuff in Belfast against the Scots four years later in 1981. My belief in him was strengthened by first-hand reports from those who had seen his performance for Middlesbrough against Sunderland in a testimonial match for goalkeeper Jim Platt. That was no exhibition affair, it was a clash between two clubs who are deadly rivals. Yet, apparently, Best not only lasted the 90 minutes but was the outstanding player on view. I guess he was just in the mood.

Even after he failed to make the Scotland game, Middlesbrough made an effort to sign him on the evidence of his performance against Sunderland. George seemed keen and then, at the last minute, decided to return to California. I imagine he couldn't face the prospect of joining a struggling side at the foot of the First Division. It is not for me to say whether his decision was right or wrong, but I'm convinced that if Best had regained peak fitness he would still have been capable of adding to the goals he scored in the First Division.

A number of those goals were scored against me, which is only to be expected since he got them against every goalkeeper in his time. My knowledge of his ability, gained at close range when we were Irish team-mates, was no protection. George could always produce the unexpected, and sell you a dummy with a swerve of his hips. I learned that the hard way on several occasions when keeping goal for Spurs against Manchester United. And one goal at White Hart Lane is still talked about by those who witnessed it.

Spurs had five players on the edge of our penalty area as George cut in from the left, and he carried the ball past each of them in a straight line before rounding the last one – Alan Mullery – and coming through the space straight at me. Then George let me make up my mind what I was going to do before wrong-footing me and slotting the ball into the net. That was Georgie.

Spurs had some good results against United, none better than in the FA Cup in January 1968 when we won a third-round replay 1–0 in extra time at White Hart Lane after the first game at Old Trafford had ended in a 2–2 draw. That replay was one of the rare occasions when I had the last laugh, for there was a moment when George got clear with only me to beat. 'Here goes,' I thought, 'this is bound to be a goal.' Imagine my delight when I won the battle of wits and snatched the ball from his toes.

One of George's favourite tricks would come when he was collecting the ball in full stride. He would go to take it with his front foot, then completely bamboozle his marker by letting the ball run and taking it with his back foot. He could do it three or four times in a match against the same opponent, and it always seemed to work.

He had so many tricks up his sleeve that when Spurs met United I was unable to offer any truly worthwhile advice to our defenders. If you told them George would do one thing, you could be sure that he'd do exactly the opposite when the time came. He had a brain which worked like lightning.

I recall one match at Old Trafford when George gave Spurs' left-back Cyril Knowles, who at that period was probably the finest full-back around, a terrible time. Cyril wasn't the type to get depressed, and when we returned to the dressing room he was ready to have a laugh at his own expense. 'That Best wasn't so hot . . .' he declared, and was about to add '. . . he was absolutely fantastic'. But Cyril never got the chance to deliver his punchline.

Bill Nicholson, Spurs' manager who wasn't noted for his sense of humour, immediately jumped in and said, 'You couldn't lace his boots, son.' Although Bill had misjudged Cyril's intention, it was a spontaneous tribute from a man who had been as dazzled as the rest of us by George.

One day George caught me on the hop when he hooked the ball away as I was preparing to kick it upfield. He went on to slip the ball into the net and the referee, who hadn't seen the incident, gave a goal.

I should have been prepared, for a week or two earlier in Belfast, playing for Northern Ireland against England, George had done exactly the same thing to Gordon Banks. On that occasion the 'goal' was disallowed, despite the indignation of George and the rest of the Irish players that it should have stood. So when Spurs met United, I might have anticipated a repeat performance – instead I was completely off-guard as I gathered the ball and went to kick it upfield.

I had the ball in my hands and could see the referee running away, with his back to me, in order to keep up with play. As I threw the ball up to kick it, George's foot came across me to intercept and control the ball all in one movement. Instinctively I had to check: if I'd followed through I would almost certainly have broken George's leg and probably my own as well. I stopped, waiting for the ref to give me the same sort of decision that Banks had got – a free-kick. But since he hadn't seen it happen, and was as baffled as most of the players on both sides, he gave a goal.

I couldn't believe it, but there wasn't much I could do about it except reflect upon the irony of the situation. I had wanted the Irish goal to stand in the international game, so I suppose I couldn't complain too much when I was on the receiving end. It was just one of those crazy inconsistencies that happen in football.

Not for the first time I was left admiring the skill, and pure cheek, of Best. I didn't go chasing after the referee, there didn't seem much point – I blamed myself for not being ready for the unexpected with George around. There were no hard feelings and we had a laugh about it after the game, but, understandably, the rest of the Spurs players were not so amused.

There was a time, when George was at odds with United, when hopes were briefly raised that Spurs might sign him – but it never materialized. What kind of fee George would have commanded can only be a matter of speculation. All I do know is that it would have been a record at the time.

I can't imagine what he would have cost when the transfer market was at its most inflated and players such as Bryan Robson, Andy Gray and Steve Daley were moving for fees in the region of £1,500,000. It is no reflection on any of that trio when I say that, by those standards, I would have to value George in the five-million class, at his peak – and a bargain at the price.

Unlike some skilful forwards, George could look after himself when the going got tough. I mentioned the power and timing of his tackling, yet although he lost his temper on occasions I never saw him go over the top at an opponent – despite the number of times he suffered that kind of treatment.

One night, playing against Bulgaria in Sofia, he took some terrible stick. It seemed the only Bulgarian tactic was to kick George at every opportunity, and they were virtually lining up to have a go at him. Finally, it was too much even for George to take and he had a kick at a defender and was sent off. What's more, Bulgaria were awarded a penalty and converted it.

The biggest tribute I can pay to George is that not a single Irish player blamed him afterwards.

13

UNITED IRELAND

Ireland should field one soccer team in international matches, including players from all 32 counties. I know that statement will infuriate a lot of people, but I make it without any political or religious bias. I am aware that a lot of administrative obstacles and a great deal of prejudice must be overcome before it is realized, but it can't be impossible. There's just one Irish XV playing Rugby Union: if the rugger types can make it work, surely the soccer authorities on both sides of the border can get together.

I thought long and hard before saying anything at all on this particular subject. In the end I decided it would be downright cowardly to avoid the issue, especially as I'm sure I have the backing of 99 per cent of Irish footballers.

I'm not swayed by any personal motives. If it ever happens, as I hope it will, it won't be until I have hung up my boots. All I know is that I'm sorry I've never had the opportunity to play for an All Ireland team at international level.

My concern is for the overall welfare of soccer in Ireland. If real progress is to be made it can only be achieved by the selection of a combined side. I'm not talking about merely qualifying for the World Cup – and Northern Ireland lead the Republic of Ireland 2–0 in that respect – but about making a real impact in the competition. If the target is to reach the semi-finals, then a united Irish team would at least double the chances.

Only twice have the two 'countries' met, home and away during the qualifying stages of the 1980 European championships. Northern Ireland drew 0–0 in Dublin and then won 1–0 in Belfast through a Gerry Armstrong goal. I took part in both matches and remember thinking, 'What the heck are we playing each other for?' – a view which must have been shared by most, if not all, of the other players.

When you consider the entire population of Ireland is around six million, it seems ridiculous to split our resources. There are more people in London, and nearly ten times as many in the whole of England, so it is small wonder that neither Irish team has ever hit the jackpot.

At the moment we are just playing percentages. Every now and again the North will produce a good all-round side; at other times it might be the turn of the South. Given complete freedom of selection, Ireland could occasionally come up with a side to challenge seriously the rest of Europe – and the world.

Northern Ireland had an exceptional side when competing in the 1958 World Cup, but I'm sure it would have been even stronger with a back-up of players from the Republic of Ireland. By contrast, the present squad in the South is clearly superior on a man-for-man assessment.

It was a crying shame the Republic did not qualify for the 1982 World Cup. They missed out in a strong group which also contained Belgium, France and Holland and were victims of some bad luck and terrible refereeing decisions in vital games. That denied players of the calibre of Liam Brady, Gerry Daly, Mark Lawrenson, David O'Leary and Frank Stapleton – not to mention promising youngsters such as Ronnie Whelan – the chance to go to Spain. They may never get another opportunity.

Just consider the names I've mentioned. All of them would have been in the running for a place in the England squad on sheer ability, and that says a lot.

Over the years the majority of the players who have represented Ireland, both North and South, wouldn't have been considered by England. In fact, on sheer resources alone, the English often could have picked ten teams stronger than anything the Irish could have produced. Usually it has been sheer team spirit, and the pride of wearing a green shirt, which has enabled Irish sides to make a game of it. But so heavily one-sided have the odds been that it is now more than 50 years since Northern Ireland beat England in Belfast.

Maybe that spirit I've mentioned has prevented either Irish team being defeated by big scores. We don't get 'murdered' like Finland, Luxembourg, Cyprus or Malta. If we did it might have prompted moves to combine.

It is impossible not to get envious when you see how well the Rugby Union link-up works. Great players such as Mike Gibson and Willie John McBride from Northern Ireland have removed the border by the manner in which they have gone into action alongside team-mates from the South. And when Ireland play at Lansdowne Road, Twickenham, Murrayfield or Cardiff Arms Park the whole nation is behind them to a man.

I don't know the exact history of the soccer split, but while Dublin was the big Rugby centre I gather that Belfast was the soccer focal-point before the formation of the original Irish Free State. That's why the Irish Football Association (North) was founded in 1880 but the Football Association of Ireland (South) didn't come into being until 1921.

The teething troubles of combining the two would, I realize, be immense and neither association would be prepared to give ground readily. There would only be one team manager and one secretary where two now exist. Flying a flag and playing a national anthem would pose all kinds of difficulties, even in ordinary times. In the current political climate, you hardly need me to spell out the problems.

Those officials who form selection committees would naturally want to hold on to their present posts, for I'm sure they all do a lot of work – and give up a vast amount of their time – for the good of soccer. You can hardly begrudge them the occasional trip abroad with an international side. Yet those are the kind of personal sacrifices needed to make a united team work successfully.

There are financial considerations as well. With only one international side, there would be less money coming into Ireland from televised matches and gate receipts; and only one Irish club would be allowed to take part in the European Cup and Cup-winners' Cup instead of the two at present.

These sorts of changes need to be accepted if Irish soccer is to make more strides in the future than it has in the past. After all, there's a lot in common between the North and South, right down to the colour of the international strips. And we do speak the same language, after a fashion.

Religious differences might be regarded as one of the major barriers, but there has always been a mixture of Protestants and Catholics in the Northern Ireland ranks. When a new player joins the squad, the only concern of the rest of us is about his ability, not which church he attends.

Nowhere is the religious influence in football more marked than in Glasgow, with the bitter rivalry between Celtic and Rangers. Yet when players from both clubs are picked for Scotland the whole country gets behind them.

Supporters, perhaps, are more conscious than players of religious differences and some of them gave me a hard time when I first earned a place in the Northern Ireland team. I thought it was a dream come true when I made my international debut at Windsor Park, but I was appalled by some of the remarks shouted at me from behind the goal.

'Go back where you belong' was the mildest form of abuse hurled in my direction.

It was a sufficient ordeal for a teenager to be playing for his country, so it was a nasty shock to find that my home crowd wasn't exactly rooting for me. The worst stick came from the staunch followers of Linfield who thought their club goalkeeper Willie McFaul – who later played for Newcastle United – should have been picked. Being a Catholic was no popularity boost.

All that is in the past. I've now been around so long that I've been accepted, or maybe the die-hards have despaired of ever getting rid of me. Even so, I felt the tension in those European championship qualifiers against the Republic of Ireland in 1980. On both occasions I was delighted to keep a clean sheet, for I knew that if I made a mistake which cost us a goal there would be plenty of remarks flying in my direction. I suppose there were those who wondered where my sympathies lie. They should have known better, for I have always been proud to represent Northern Ireland.

The security forces on both sides of the border were clearly concerned about the possibility of trouble when the two European ties were staged, but, fortunately, there was only one incident which might have provoked a flare-up. That was in Belfast when some idiot threw a stone which laid out the Republic of Ireland mid-field man Gerry Daly.

It was a crazy thing to do – how did the missile-thrower know he wouldn't hit a home player? – and Gerry earned a lot of credit for the way he reacted. He went off to have the wound stitched and came back to play as if nothing had happened. He didn't make a fuss at the time, and he didn't complain afterwards. If it had been a continental footballer instead of Daly, the victim might understandably have kicked up a song and dance and caused all kinds of repercussions – not least of all causing UEFA to act and perhaps close Windsor Park.

The fact that players from both the North and South get on well together was underlined for me when I travelled to Dublin to play for a combined side which, under the label of Shamrock Rovers, met Brazil in a charity game. There was a balance of Catholics and Protestants and it was the companionship of that night which first got me thinking we ought to get together at full international level.

I can only repeat that I think it would work on the field if the behind-the-scenes situation could be sorted out. And while it wouldn't benefit me, it could forge one side capable of giving any nation in the world a game, and perhaps prevent another outstanding player like George

Best going right through his career without having the opportunity to parade his talents in a World Cup.

Let me turn now to another international topic which has sparked off considerable controversy: the qualification rules regarding the selection of players for a country. I know a lot of English fans feel that the Irish, Scots and Welsh have gained a big advantage in this respect since ruling body FIFA altered the system.

In the old days a footballer could only play for the country in which he had been born. One of the most famous Welsh full-backs, Walley Barnes of Arsenal, was really an Englishman who first saw the light of day in Wales because his father was stationed there in the Army at the time. The anomalies of the old system can be seen when you find brothers playing for different countries. John Hollins won an England cap while his elder brother David, a goalkeeper, represented Wales. Most ironical of all, Joe Baker played for England and his brother Gerry played for the United States, whilst they were really Scots with a truly tartan accent.

If Joe, a free-scoring centre-forward who played for Hibs, Arsenal, Nottingham Forest and Sunderland, had been given the choice I'm sure he would have elected to play for Scotland. So I favour the existing rule, whereby players are selected on the basis of their nationality.

Ron Greenwood might understandably have taken the opposite view when he was England manager. The old rule would have enabled David O'Leary and Mark Lawrenson, the Republic of Ireland centre-backs, to have played for him in the 1982 World Cup since both were born in England.

I think the nationality of parents provides a stronger qualification than the place of birth. Three of my four children were born in England but I regard them as Irish. But for the change of rule the wives of many Irish, Scots and Welsh footballers with English clubs would travel home for the birth of their children to safeguard their nationality.

I've always found that English-born players who qualified for Northern Ireland were every bit as enthusiastic and patriotic. A classic example is centre-half Chris Nicholl, who has always stretched himself to the limit in his games in an Irish shirt.

Big Chris made a relatively late entry into the international arena. So far as I know he was never considered by England, perhaps because he spent part of his career with Aston Villa in the Second and Third Divisions, and for a long time the Irish FA didn't realize he was eligible to play for Northern Ireland.

I rated the combination of Chris and Allan Hunter the best central-defence partnership I've played behind in an Irish team. They dove-tailed well with each other, and I never had to worry if the opposition had a couple of six-footers in attack if Chris and Allan were around to look after them.

Hunter gave such splendid service it was a pity that injury took its toll and prevented him playing in the 1980 British championship when Northern Ireland surprised everybody by winning the title with five points out of a possible six. It was a fairly memorable way to celebrate the centenary of the Irish FA.

By a touch of irony, I missed sharing in that triumph after waiting for so many years for it to happen. So did first-choice full-backs Pat Rice and Sammy Nelson. Arsenal couldn't release any of us because, immediately after the FA Cup final against West Ham, we were wanted for the European Cup-winners' Cup final with Valencia in Spain. Manager Terry Neill felt it would be foolish to risk any injuries, and Pat, Sammy and I naturally accepted the situation.

It was a big disappointment to me to be absent from that victorious Irish side, but my replacement Jim Platt had three fine games. Perhaps the fact that Northern Ireland were below full-strength helped in an odd way to make the Scots and English overconfident.

Northern Ireland began with a 1–0 Belfast success against Scotland, followed up with a deserved 1–1 Wembley draw with England and then clinched the title by beating Wales 1–0. As the results indicated, the Irish defence was excellent – and Nicholl was outstanding.

Even without playing, I was proud of that Irish achievement. I knew just how much it meant to the lads in the team and all the Irish officials after being regarded as under-dogs for so long. Let's be honest about it. The Irish and Welsh are treated as second-class citizens in the British championship, just there to make the numbers up. That's why the game between those two countries is usually staged on a Friday night before the 'big match' between England and Scotland at Wembley or Hampden Park.

Yet Northern Ireland's success wasn't such a surprise to me. We had proved we had the nucleus of a good side by finishing as runners-up to England in our European championship qualifying group, and the return of Billy Bingham to take over as manager added a fresh impetus – just as the appointment of a new boss often revitalizes a club team.

Bingham is a sound tactician, and I think the playing style he adopts is that which best suits Northern Ireland. He knows our strength lies in good organization with the emphasis on stopping the other side rather than trying to match them in all aspects of the game. Billy favours playing from the back – and hitting on the break. He accepts Northern Ireland aren't likely to score many goals, so if we get one he wants to make it count. Those are the tactics which paid off in 1980.

Danny Blanchflower, by contrast, always demanded more flair. He wanted his team to perform like the Spurs 'double' side he had captained in 1960–61, to go at the opposition at every opportunity even if pushing forward usually resulted in losing possession. We tried to do it that way – for Danny's sake – but the cruel truth is that the Irish team wasn't equipped to make it work. Although I used to argue the point with him, I have the greatest admiration for Danny – a smashing bloke with the interests of football and the fans at heart.

If Bingham is a realist, Blanchflower was a dreamer so far as Northern Ireland was concerned. He believes the game is about enjoyment for the players and entertainment for the spectators, and he wanted to recreate the kind of Irish side which Peter Doherty had guided to the World Cup in 1958. He felt Peter had done a marvellous job for Northern Ireland and hoped to do the same. Unfortunately, he lacked the players to make his dream come true.

One night everything did come together, when we drew 2–2 in Holland against a star-studded Dutch side. That was the highlight of Danny's spell in charge – Northern Ireland produced his kind of football for 90 magical minutes.

Danny didn't drink or smoke, yet he could certainly talk. I could listen to him for hours and often did: he's a great thinker about the game and has some fairly revolutionary ideas. One idea he had was to try and baffle the opposition when they gained a corner-kick by keeping five of our players up on the half-way line. 'Let's see what they do,' he would say; 'perhaps they will keep five or six men back to look after you.'

Another suggestion of his was that we shouldn't form a wall if opponents were awarded a free-kick 25 yards out. I wasn't so keen on that plan. Giving international players a clear shot at goal is a dangerous business, even from that range. I told him I'd end up with a sore back from picking the ball out of the net.

One great advantage when Danny was manager was that he took all the pressure off the players by dealing with the media. 'I'll make the excuses when we lose,' he used to say, 'but you better have some good excuses for me.'

He was a God-send to the Irish journalists, who have a fairly thankless task. When we are beaten by a superior side they have to come up with an in-depth analysis of what has gone wrong, judge the performances of individual players and suggest changes. Yet they know that the real reason is limited resources and the lack of enough players of the required calibre. They would certainly have more scope if there was an all-Ireland team.

I've played under other Irish managers. The first was Bertie Peacock who, like Danny, had been a talented wing-half in his own playing days. When he joined in training spells you got some idea of just how good a player Bertie must have been in his heyday with Celtic. He was a down-to-earth fellow, who never stood for any nonsense and was respected by all the players. Bertie never pulled any punches. He would be absolutely straight with you, say exactly what he wanted and usually get it. There's no doubt in my mind that Bertie would have been a big success at club or international level had he decided to stay in management, but business commitments influenced him to resign the Irish job.

Dave Clements had a year or so in charge, bridging the gap between Terry Neill and Danny Blanchflower. I felt the odds were against Dave at the beginning, for he had to handle men with whom he had been playing. To his credit, he overcame that obstacle and I thought he would have a bright future, but then he went to the United States. He used to fly home for international games but it soon became obvious the arrangement could not work in the long term.

Judged on results there's no doubt that Billy Bingham has been Northern Ireland's most successful manager since Peter Doherty. Now, in his second spell in the job, he has more authority in his dealings with players because of his extra experience. He seems to have acquired a greater presence.

Billy likes to show he's the boss in every respect, even when it comes to ordering meals for the players. He feels he knows just what is best for them to eat and – though there may be an occasional moan – the lads accept his menu in the same way that they adhere to his tactics. Footballers generally like to play for a manager with a mind of his own, because it instils confidence in them. So I've got no complaints with Billy, except that I wish he wouldn't order so many salads.

I've won more caps for my country than any other footballer, but Northern Ireland lost the most valuable member of our international squad early in the 1981–82 season when trainer Bobby McGregor collapsed and died in Sofia, Bulgaria, during a European Cup-tie. And I lost a real friend. A smashing, warm-hearted fellow who was always ready to do anybody a good turn.

To use the official term and label Bobby as 'trainer' hardly does justice to his memory. He was the finest physiotherapist in the game – a view which I'm sure would be endorsed by every Irish player without the slightest disrespect to the men who have treated them for injuries at club level. Bobby had magic fingers, and years of experience supplementing a God-given gift.

I suppose, in a way, it was appropriate that Bobby died doing the job he loved best. He was on duty with his club Glentoran for a match against Bulgarian champions CSKA and was actually on the field treating an injured player, offering his usual words of encouragement, when he collapsed.

Glentoran were knocked out of the European Cup that night, but I'm told there were tears in the dressing room after the game which had nothing to do with the result. Bobby's death overshadowed everything else, and I can understand the team's feeling of loss. It hit me just as hard at home when the news came through on the radio.

I could hardly believe my ears, and when my wife Eleanor came running down the stairs I needed only one look at her face to know that she too had heard the sad news. Our first thoughts were for Bobby's family back in Belfast, his wife Winnie and sons Colin and Trevor.

It seemed like the end of an era for me. Bobby had been the Northern Ireland physio for 12 years, and during that time I owed him a great deal for getting me fit for international matches. More than once I reported for a game wondering whether I'd be able to play – but once I'd had the McGregor treatment there was no problem. In fact, after Bobby had worked on me for five minutes I felt I could jump over the crossbar. He was that good.

I can remember more than one occasion when I landed on the back of my neck after leaping to catch a cross into the goalmouth. In a matter of minutes my neck would feel as stiff as a board, but a quick massage from Bobby would soon have it as right as rain. Whatever the injury, he could put his finger on it instantly.

If he told you an injury was 'hopeless' then you didn't waste time with a second opinion. But it was rare for him to admit defeat.

Before a Northern Ireland game, there was always a player who would limp into the hotel when the party reported. One look at his twisted ankle or swollen knee would have the rest of us agreeing there was no chance of playing two or three days later. Then Bobby would go into action and the difference would have to be seen to be believed. The casualty would be fit, strapped up and getting through 90 minutes without complaint. After the match one would read that the same player wasn't fit for his club for the next couple of weeks because he didn't have a Bobby McGregor to treat him. I've no doubt that a number of players who have been finished by injury would have lasted a lot longer had they known Bobby.

Apart from being constantly cheerful, and always ready to put a comforting arm round your shoulders if you'd had a poor game and convince you it wasn't really your fault, he was such a meticulous man. He insisted upon giving each player a rub down after every training session because he believed it was part of his job. In that way he could often 'feel' an injury coming on and avoid serious trouble.

Bobby's reputation was a legend throughout Northern Ireland. Although Glentoran trainer, he was always being asked to treat players of rival Irish League clubs and never turned anybody away. He was Glentoran through and through – he had several spells as manager but wasn't interested in the job permanently – yet his nature was such that he must have spent many hours getting footballers from other clubs fit to play against them.

When Spurs centre-half Mike England was out of action for ages with a troublesome injury, I suggested that he went over to Belfast to see Bobby. Mike soon regained full fitness and later, when team manager of Wales, he would ask Bobby's advice if one of his players had a long-term injury.

Rugby Union star Mike Gibson has also said that he would never have played so many internationals for Ireland but for Bobby's help. And, incredibly, Bobby told me that he had even treated greyhounds, who apparently can have the same muscular problems as footballers.

Bobby's medical career started when he joined the Red Cross as a teenager. At his place of work he spent most of his lunch hour treating everybody with bad backs, from the boss downwards. So it was hardly surprising when he eventually branched out and opened his own clinic.

There, I'm told, the queues used to form by nine o'clock in the morning and he would be kept busy until long after dark. He welcomed anybody: those who couldn't afford to pay still got the treatment and were told to forget the debt until their boat came in. He made a good living and it never bothered him that he might have made a great deal more if he'd chosen to move across the water to England.

Bobby's one passion, outside the hobby which became his work, was fast cars. I recall when he was the proud owner of one of the very first Jaguar XJ12s in Ireland. I was in Belfast for a Friday night international match against Wales, and afterwards he took me to his home to show me his prized possession. When I admired the car – and it was a beauty – Bobby handed me the keys and insisted I borrow it for a few days to go home to Newry. That was an absolutely typical gesture.

Mr Jack Balmer, an eminent surgeon who accompanies the Northern Ireland team, once said of Bobby, 'When he dies it's a tragic waste to think that his methods will be lost.' He was so right. But the loss of the man himself was an even bigger tragedy to all of us who were privileged to regard him as a friend.

14

WORLD CUP EUPHORIA

I thought I'd been around the football scene far too long to get emotional over the result of any match, but I've got to admit I had a lump in my throat when the final whistle sounded at Valencia's beautiful Luis Casanova Stadium around eleven o'clock on the night of Friday, 25 June 1982. Northern Ireland had beaten host-nation Spain 1–0 to win Group Five of the 1982 World Cup, and become one of the 12 countries to qualify for the second stage of the competition, before the eyes of a disbelieving crowd of 49,000.

It was a result nobody had forecast, and I stood on the pitch wondering if it had really happened. All around me the other Irish lads were hugging each other in mutual congratulation, and I still have a mental picture of manager Billy Bingham and goalscorer Gerry Armstrong locked in an embrace on the touchline.

I have played in many better teams in my time, but I've never been as proud to be a member of any side than I was at that moment. No words can really convey my feelings. It wasn't just national pride. It was a sense of belonging, of being part of something special.

Northern Ireland used 13 players in that game, including substitutes Tommy Cassidy and Sammy Nelson, and each one had contributed in full to the success. And I'm not forgetting left-back Mal Donaghy, who had been sent off 30 minutes from the end. Mal was the victim of a harsh decision after pushing Spain's Camacho away in self-protection as they tangled on the touchline.

Nothing in soccer has given me greater satisfaction than victory in Valencia. I didn't want to leave the pitch when it was all over, and, in fact, I think I was the last player to do so after giving an on-the-spot interview to BBC television.

The Irish team had started the World Cup as 150–1 outsiders. We went into action against Spain after drawing our two previous matches, 0–0 with Yugoslavia and 1–1 with Honduras, and with our flight tickets home already booked for two days later. We knew we had to win to avoid elimination – even a goalless draw wouldn't be enough to save us. Some of the lads had their bags packed in readiness for the journey back.

There was the possibility that if we drew by 2–2 or more we would progress, but that hardly seemed likely after scoring just once in two matches. To be honest, it seemed a heck of a long shot.

It's true the Spaniards hadn't been very impressive in their earlier group fixtures, yet they had the backing of a capacity crowd noted for its noisy enthusiasm. Every one of their supporters seemed to be waving a flag and I can't remember experiencing an atmosphere which compared with that night.

Footballers will tell you that there are games when it seems the gods are on your side, when your team can do no wrong. Northern Ireland had one of those games against Spain.

I wasn't overworked, but I was aware that if I conceded an early goal Spanish morale would soar sky-high and we might be over-whelmed. So I was pleased with a save I made at the feet of Ufarte in the opening minutes.

When we reached half-time with the scoresheet blank, our hopes of creating a sensation began to rise. And when Armstrong put us ahead two minutes into the second half, after he had combined with Billy Hamilton to open up the Spanish defence, everything suddenly seemed possible. Admittedly, events took a turn for the worse on the hour when the luckless Donaghy was shown the red card on the say-so of a Peruvian linesman. But that was when true Irish fighting spirit came to the surface and the Spaniards became more and more frustrated.

Although under constant pressure in the closing stages, we were worried more by the referee than the Spanish players. The fear that he might award a penalty against us was uppermost in our minds. We had seen Spain get doubtful penalties in both their previous matches, and the last thing we wanted was to be the fall guys for a hat-trick. I was certainly thinking that way when the Spaniards had their final fling for an equalizer as the game went into injury time, and the ball bounced a yard in front of me with Juanito rushing in for the kill.

I could see the ball was too high for Juanito to reach, and I sensed that if I made contact with him I might be penalized and the game could slip from out grasp. So I knew exactly what I was doing when I tipped the ball over his head and dived to retrieve it. Later I was told that millions of viewers, watching the match on TV all over Britain, had their hearts in their mouths at that instant. I can only repeat that, however it looked, I had the situation under control.

As it happened, the referee did whistle – and awarded us a free-kick. Whether he would have made the same decision, and risked the wrath of the frenzied fans, if the ball had gone into the net is one of those questions I'm glad will forever go unanswered.

The ref, Senor Ortiz from Paraguay, must have been under tremendous pressure. Whenever I got the ball in the last 15 minutes he warned me not to waste time, so it's still something of a mystery why he added on three minutes at the finish.

I have told you of my elation when the final whistle blew, but to appreciate it to the full you have to realize that for months I had my doubts whether I would be picked for Northern Ireland's World Cup squad – let alone the team. My nightmare about missing soccer's greatest event, after waiting 19 years for my World Cup chance, had begun on Saturday, 2 January 1982 – of all days, my 15th wedding anniversary – when I suffered a severe groin injury in a Spurs–Arsenal third-round FA Cup-tie.

It was five weeks before I was fit enough even to have a run out in Arsenal's reserve team, but it looked as if I was on the mend and Billy Bingham picked me to play for Northern Ireland against England at Wembley at the end of February. As usually seems to happen when we meet England, we didn't get any of the breaks which were going and lost 4–0. But it wasn't all bad from my point of view. I made several good saves and left the field convinced that my injury worries were behind me.

A week or so later, disaster struck. The BBC had decided to produce a 35-minute documentary on my career, and it was during the filming at Arsenal's training ground at London Colney that I again tore my groin. I was demonstrating a drop-kick, something I had been doing regularly, when it happened.

I don't think I have ever felt so sorry for myself as I did when the realization set in that I faced a race against time to fulfil my World Cup ambition. And as the weeks went by I began to panic that I wouldn't make it to Spain.

March and April passed and I missed two Northern Ireland games, Jim Platt taking over in goal for the 4–0 defeat by France in Paris and a 1–1 draw with Scotland in Belfast. The match against Wales at Wrexham at the end of May represented my last hope of getting back into the reckoning. It wasn't regarded by the public as the most important international fixture of all time, for the crowd of 2,315 was the lowest ever recorded for a game in the British championship series. But it was vital so far as I was concerned, a make-or-break affair.

Manager Bingham must have given a lot of thought to the matter as he debated whether or not to pick me. Eventually, he decided to give me 45 minutes – but, to be on the safe side, he played me in the first half so that Platt was on stand-by to take over for the rest of the match if I broke down. Touch wood, it was all right on the night. When I came off at the interval with Wales 1–0 ahead – they ultimately won 3–0 – I was happier than I'd been for ages. The first hurdle had been surmounted, and I felt I would be in Bingham's World Cup squad of 22.

I have to be honest and admit that I wasn't confident I would be the Irish first choice in Spain. Since Platt had been playing regularly for Middlesbrough while I'd been on the injured list, I could hardly have complained if he had got the nod. In fact, at that time I would have settled for just one match in the World Cup.

Something quite unforeseen cast a doubt whether Jim or I would even get to Spain. War broke out following the invasion of the Falkland Islands by Argentina, and there was a strong possibility that the British government would order England, Scotland and Northern Ireland to withdraw from the World Cup.

There was no question of Argentina being banned from the competition. They were holders of the trophy and it was quite clear that Spanish sympathy was on the side of the South Americans.

It has been recorded that it was Prime Minister Margaret Thatcher's decision to allow the three British teams to take part in the World Cup, despite opposition from several members of the Cabinet. I certainly wanted to go to Spain, yet felt it would have been understandable if Mrs Thatcher had decreed otherwise. The thought of playing football against Argentina when young men from both countries were killing each other would have been ludicrous.

Fortunately, victory for Britain in the Falklands came the day following the World Cup kick-off. Argentina lost three of their five games in Spain and returned home with their morale shattered.

Whilst the Argentinian squad had been together for three months, Northern Ireland's footballers did not assemble until a fortnight before the World Cup began. We actually flew to Spain on the very day the opening match was played in Barcelona.

Our squad of 22 toned up at Brighton. It may not sound the most exotic of places, but it proved an ideal choice on the part of Billy Bingham. We were in familiar surroundings, with no food worries or language problems, and the weather during the first two weeks in June was so hot it was perfect preparation for what we could expect in Spain. We all had a healthy tan before we arrived in Valencia.

Billy soon made it clear that Brighton was to be no holiday. He worked us morning and afternoon and it was as tough as pre-season training. We wondered what had hit us as we pounded out lap after lap and went on rigorous cross-country runs. Some of the lads grumbled, as footballers always do, yet the policy undoubtedly paid off when we came to play in the Spanish heat. Northern Ireland may not have been the most skilful side in the World Cup, but we proved second to none when it came to fitness in the demanding conditions.

I certainly felt a hundred per cent after my crash course at Brighton, and it was hard to believe that just a couple of weeks earlier I'd had so many misgivings about my fitness. Jim Platt looked sharp as well, and I still wasn't sure whether I'd be picked. He must have been disappointed when Billy Bingham announced that I would be in the team.

Jim never said anything at the time, but on the eve of our third match with Spain the newspapers ran a story that he felt that he should have been Northern Ireland's first choice and that he'd had a rough deal. I didn't know a thing about it until after I had returned home at the end of the tournament, and even now I think that either Jim was misquoted or some of what he said was taken out of context. He isn't a moaner and there has never been any ill feeling between us.

It may well have been that, like the rest of us, he thought we would be on our way home after the Spain game and that he would be deprived of playing in the World Cup. But his timing was terrible, especially as I'd come smoothly through the two opening matches.

Things have a funny way of working out in football. Having beaten Spain, I felt a reaction to my groin injury and missed the next match – against Austria in Madrid at the start of the second series. So Jim got his chance. Even though it was at my expense, I was genuinely glad Platt was able to play that one game. He'd been in my shadow for years and I can understand the frustration he would have felt if he'd missed appearing in the World Cup – especially as it could be quite a while before Northern Ireland qualify again.

When the squad reported at Brighton, Bingham had emphasized that he had an open mind about the composition of the team, stressing that nobody could be sure of a place and that the opportunity was there for any of the 22 who impressed him during the build-up. It was a challenge to the younger and less experienced members of the squad, even if it was obvious that only two or three positions – including goalkeeper – were really up for grabs. Some of the lads in the party knew it was unlikely they would get any nearer to the action than the substitutes' bench.

One player who took Bingham at his word and forced his way into the team was Norman Whiteside of Manchester United, who because of his World Cup exploits and his subsequent club form is now a household name in the game. When we reported at Brighton young Norman was still an unknown, not long past his 17th birthday with just a single First Division appearance for United to his credit. What's more, he had not long recovered from a cartilage operation.

Norman was a revelation – that's the only way I can do justice to the impact he made. He looked so big and strong it was difficult to believe he was just a kid and still growing – for the sake of the rest of the First Division, I hope he stops soon.

He's a quiet lad, so I'm sure the instant fame will not go to his head. Comparisons with George Best are ridiculous – they are as different as chalk and cheese – but there's no doubt Norman has a great future. If I had to nominate a footballer of the eighties at this stage, my money would have to be on Whiteside. In addition to his size and strength, he has an educated left foot.

It was clear after the first couple of days training at Brighton that Norman would be in the running for a World Cup place. In fact, he played in all five Northern Ireland games – and when he was substituted in the latter stages of three of them it was only because the boss was being protective in view of Norman's tender years.

Not that Norman couldn't take care of himself. He soon showed he wasn't going to let anybody push him around, and in the very first match against Yugoslavia he was booked.

Norman's influence in Spain had a lot to do with our success because the Irish team had previously lacked attacking power. Suddenly we had Billy Hamilton as the spearhead with Whiteside on his left and Gerry Armstrong allowed greater scope on the right, able to drop slightly deeper and run at opponents. What Northern Ireland achieved in Spain was the result of team effort, but I'm sure the rest of the lads will agree with me that we owed a lot to the 'Three Musketeers' up front – Armstrong, Hamilton and Whiteside.

It's incredible when you think about it. Armstrong had spent much of the previous season as Watford substitute as my old club gained promotion from the Second Division. Hamilton has been playing in the Third Division with another side which was promoted, Burnley. Whiteside had just 90 minutes' League football behind him. Yet, in my view, they did as well as any attacking trio from any of the 24 World Cup countries because they had one thing in common – a big heart.

Hamilton didn't get the recognition he deserved, for he did a hell of a job for us. Billy's a big, awkward fellow who took a physical battering in every game without a murmur of complaint. He is probably best remembered for the way he hurdled a tackle and provided the cross for Armstrong to get that memorable winner against Spain, but Billy got a couple of goals himself in the 2–2 draw with Austria in the second series. One was a header after a spectacular run by Armstrong which must rate among the finest goals of the tournament.

Gerry Armstrong – what is there left to say about him? I'm just delighted that Gerry virtually became a star overnight, and was voted the outstanding British player in the World Cup. It couldn't have happened to a nicer fellow.

Gerry is one of those super-fit players who can run for days without appearing to stop for breath. He's prepared to give his last drop of blood, and even if things aren't going well for him is the type who never stops trying.

Since George Best disappeared from the international scene, Gerry has been my room-mate on Northern Ireland trips. In the past, he had spent a lot of time answering telephone calls for me, taking messages when I wasn't around or making excuses if I was resting. In Spain the roles were reversed. It was Gerry who was in constant demand – from Press, TV and newly-found friends – and I found myself acting as his secretary.

Maybe it was because of the possibilities of our new attacking formation, plus my own rising confidence at regaining full fitness, that as we travelled to Spain I started to feel for the first time Northern Ireland could finish in one of the two top places in Group Five. The team could hardly have had a more dismal record, since our four internationals in 1982 had ended in three defeats and a draw: we had scored only one goal and conceded 12. A month before we left for Spain it looked as if we were just going to be there to make up the numbers. There was a danger we might even be humiliated. But Billy Bingham had done a splendid job boosting morale, and I suddenly thought we could – with a bit of luck – creep into second place behind Spain.

As host country I had assumed the Spaniards would dominate the group and there was a tendency to discount Honduras. That feeling soon disappeared when we saw films of the Central American team playing in their qualifying matches. We realized Honduras would be anything but a soft touch.

That much was confirmed when, the night before our opener with Yugoslavia, we saw Honduras 'live'. They drew 1–1 with Spain and were robbed of victory by a home-town penalty. Honduras had four or five players who wouldn't have looked out of place in some of the more highly rated World Cup teams, and they had an excellent goal-keeper in Arzu.

I was particularly impressed with their composure in that first game, for the screaming of 49,000 Spanish fans would have unnerved a lot of sides. Even when Spain got that lucky penalty equalizer, with 25 minutes left, the Honduras players kept their cool in difficult circumstances.

The Irish team watched that game with mixed feelings. We were all instinctively on the side of the under-dogs, coming into that same category ourselves, but the quality of the Honduras performance underlined that we were going to have three difficult group games instead of two. It made it absolutely vital that we didn't lose our opening encounter with the Yugoslavs at the La Romareda Stadium in Zaragoza, even though our opponents would start red-hot favourites.

Yugoslavia had a formidable line-up containing some of the most talented footballers in Europe, and a manager, Miljan Miljanic, who is renowned as a master tactician. Since Yugoslavia had a long, un-beaten run of games behind them it looked certain we faced a backs-to-the-wall assignment. Our plan had to be to get as many players as possible behind the ball, avoid foolish errors in our own half of the field and try to hit them on the break.

In terms of reputation, Miljanic had more talented players on the bench than Bingham had on the field. But once again Billy got it right, because in his pre-match tactical talk he made it clear he was more concerned with the way we played than with the individual ability of the Yugoslavs. 'We'll be OK if we do our job properly,' he stressed.

That's how things turned out, for not only did we get a goalless draw but we fully deserved it on the night. Our fitness was a plus in the steaming heat of Zaragoza – even with an eight o'clock kick-off the sweat was dripping off us in a matter of minutes – and we lasted the pace far better than the Yugoslavs.

I was satisfied with my own display. I made a couple of saves, nothing very special but still satisfying after my lengthy lay-off from top-class football.

Whilst delighted with the result, I was disappointed with the Yugoslavs. I'd expected a great deal more of them, but most of their players appeared to be ready to settle for a point well before the end. In fact, they looked thankful to get it. Yugoslavia didn't improve in the next match and lost 2–1 to Spain. It was a good result for Northern Ireland, for we knew that victory over Honduras in Zaragoza would give us a wonderful chance of going on to Madrid as one of the élite.

An early goal by Armstrong in the Honduras match was just the tonic we needed, but in the end we couldn't complain when Laing equalized with a header in the 60th minute and the game ended 1–1. Honduras gave us more problems than either of the more illustrious rivals in the group.

I was upset by the Honduras goal since it came from a corner after I had made a good save from a close-range header. But later in the match I made my finest save of the World Cup, diving full-length to turn a shot round the post with my fingertips. To my amazement, and to the annoyance of the Honduras players, the referee – a gentleman from Hong Kong called Chen Tam Sun – promptly awarded a goal-kick. He had not realized that I'd reached the ball, even though it must have been apparent to the millions watching on TV.

I was happy enough the referee got it wrong. I wasn't looking for personal glory at that moment, and was relieved to avoid the risk of Honduras getting another goal from a corner-kick.

We flew back to our hotel in Valencia feeling somewhat deflated by the result. Whatever the permutations if we drew our last match with Spain, the realistic view was that victory was the only way of guaranteeing our progress. And that seemed too big a task.

That's why Northern Ireland's 1–0 win when the crunch came was such an intoxicating feeling, even to an old-timer like me. Footballers are accustomed to being told 'a team is only as good as its last performance'. As we celebrated in the dressing room on that never-to-be-forgotten night we felt like the best team in the world.

Skipper Martin O'Neill, asked by a TV interviewer 'What will you do now?' came up with the only possible reply. 'We'll probably win the World Cup,' declared Martin. Any outsider present as the champagne flowed in our hotel in Valencia a few hours later would have thought that we had already won it.

Even the Spanish staff and our posse of security guards – we had two favourite massive minders whom we nicknamed Starsky and Hutch – joined in the carnival spirit back at the hotel. They were all Irish that night and the locals seemed genuinely pleased at our triumph. Perhaps the fact that Spain had also qualified for the next stage, as group runners-up, had softened the blow.

The setting was right for the celebrations, for our stay at that hotel at Valencia had us in relaxed mood from the very moment we checked in. It was in an ideal location, right on the beach with two swimming pools and a couple of tennis courts.

We did our share of sunbathing, which seemed to surprise a lot of people when other teams in Spain were banned by their managers from sitting in the sun. Billy Bingham took the opposite view, and after morning training and an afternoon sleep each day he allowed us to sunbathe for an hour or so. He felt that it could do us no harm and it certainly prevented any boredom, for the alternative would have been to sit around in our rooms and watch TV.

The news that we were enjoying ourselves got out of hand, for the Spanish papers soon had lurid stories that the Irish players were either drinking or dancing at the local disco most of the time. We all had a good laugh when we learned what was being written about us, but we were thankful the British press lads who were staying at the same hotel could put the record straight.

The truth was that we were all too aware of what was at stake in the World Cup to step out of line, and prior to beating Spain none of the players had more than an occasional drink – and then only after a game. We knew that if any of us were seen having a couple of lagers the word would get around we'd had nine or ten.

Perhaps the object of those stories was to upset our team spirit before the game with Spain . . . such tactics are not unknown abroad. But whatever the reason, and whether the reports were malicious or just misguided, the Northern Ireland players had the last laugh. When the Spanish reporters turned up at the hotel after our 1–0 win, one of our lads took them gently aside and said, 'Just imagine what the score would have been if we'd stayed sober.'

15

SO NEAR
AND YET SO FAR

Little Northern Ireland, the no-hopers of the tournament, reached the second stage of the World Cup along with Argentina, Austria, Belgium, Brazil, England, France, Italy, Poland, Russia, Spain and West Germany. While the players of the other 11 countries must have fancied their chances of progressing that far, we had travelled with no greater objective than to give a reasonable account of ourselves.

If there was a secret to our success it was the togetherness of the whole party. So far as the players were concerned, we had no stars or prima donnas.

I think one decision helped to promote the spirit amongst the squad: we agreed before arriving in Spain that all payments would be divided 22 ways. There was a sliding scale of £600 apiece for the 11 players in the team, £400 each for the five substitutes and £200 for the other six lads. But we decided unanimously that it should be pooled and then divided equally.

At the final count it meant that the five who didn't kick a ball – Bobby Campbell, Jim Cleary, George Dunlop, Tom Finney and Johnny Jameson – got exactly the same bonus as the five who were on the pitch for every minute of each game, Gerry Armstrong, Billy Hamilton, Chris Nicholl, Jimmy Nicholl and John McClelland. It worked out at more than £5,000 a man. The four Irish League players, all part-timers who earn only peanuts from football, were particularly pleased with the reward. And I was especially delighted for our third-choice goalkeeper George Dunlop, of Linfield, who had been made redundant from his full-time job in Belfast shortly before the World Cup.

After Northern Ireland had qualified for the World Cup, the players were accused of being greedy when we protested at the cash offered to us in Spain. We were told to count our blessings with so many people out of work. It was an understandable reaction, but we felt the initial offer of the Irish FA was penny-pinching and we wanted to make our point.

In many respects, it was a typical example of Irish organization, for the situation arose from confusion rather than ill-feeling. As an example, the offer we received didn't even mention payment for matches in the second stage. Nobody on the Irish FA had really expected us to get that far. Eventually the powers that be decided to contact the Scottish FA and put us on exactly the same scale of pay as the Scots.

The fact that we upset the odds by winning our first group brought another problem when we eventually moved on to Madrid. Officials of the other countries had sent representatives to the Spanish capital a few months in advance to inspect the hotels allocated by ruling body FIFA and state their preference. Northern Ireland hadn't bothered – so we ended up with the last one on the list.

I don't want to pile on the agony, it wasn't run-down or third rate. Far from it. The rooms were spacious, the food was superb and the staff couldn't have been more friendly and helpful. But while Spain and England went to country retreats, set in acres of land with swimming pools and training pitches, we found ourselves in a typical airport hotel with absolutely no facilities for a football team. The windows were treble glazed, to keep out the noise of passing aircraft, and everywhere was darkened to combat the stifling heat. It seemed like the middle of the night all the time.

Once we had finished training there was absolutely nothing for us to do except laze around in our rooms. It would have been better if we had remained in Valencia and flown to Madrid for the games with Austria and France. After all, we had flown to Zaragoza for two matches in the first stage and the flight time to Madrid wasn't much more. But it was too late to change the hotel, so we all had a moan and then made the best of things. We had a couple of outings to a local swimming pool to break the monotony, but it was so crowded it was like the beach at Brighton or Blackpool on a Bank Holiday.

While the other teams had private training pitches, we went to the ground of a small club just outside Madrid each day – and hundreds of children turned up to watch us. That was OK with us, we got on well with them and signed autographs non-stop, but it did lead to one unfortunate incident.

Some of the children, like kids the world over, used to watch shooting practice and when a ball came their way they would go off for a game of their own. We were forever chasing them to retrieve the balls. One little lad was a bit cheeky and John O'Neill made as if to kick the ball at him. A Spaniard, standing some distance away, mistakenly thought the boy had been hit and ran on to the pitch shouting abuse. In a flash he was intercepted by the security guards and whipped away, but not before the whole drama had been recorded by the TV cameras.

None of the players gave the affair another thought, so it was annoying to learn later it had been shown on television all over Europe. It was a classic case of making a mountain out of a molehill, but it was one of those things which could have been avoided if the Northern Ireland party had been in a more suitable hotel.

It was a particular pity because I thought the entire organization of the World Cup was a credit to the Spaniards. The pitches were immaculate, the timing of travel and kick-offs was perfect, with no hassle or infuriating delays, and we couldn't have been made more welcome.

The only real hold-up came at the end of each game, but that was due to what I can best describe as 'natural causes'. Two players from each side were taken away for the routine drug test, and were required to give a sample of their urine.

This would be no bother on a cold day in Britain, but it was a different story in the sizzling heat of Spain. Players lost so much sweat that on average they shed eight or nine pounds in weight. So it often took two hours to do as the doctor ordered and fill a bottle.

The rest of us hung around – thank goodness, I was never called upon for a test – until our team-mates reappeared. And they were usually in merry mood, having been supplied with beer and lager to help them oblige. When Northern Ireland played in Zaragoza, and then had to fly back to Valencia, the charter plane was inevitably delayed until well after midnight.

I believe the record time for a drug test was four hours, involving an unfortunate Brazilian. His team-mates went off and left him at the stadium!

There was one other irritation you don't encounter in the First Division, for the heat was such that each time the ball bounced on the grass it caused thousands of midges to swarm up. They got in your eyes and down your throat and it was fairly unpleasant.

In our first group we had played at night, but when we got to Madrid to do battle with Austria and France for a semi-final spot our games were in the heat of the afternoon to fit into the TV schedule. Not that we cared: being there was what mattered.

The programme was in our favour in Group D because we had the opportunity to see Austria and France in opposition in the opening match. That game in the Vicente Calderon Stadium left the entire Irish squad in no doubt that the French were the more formidable side.

The form of the French in their opening group in the north of

Spain, when they met England, Kuwait and Czechoslovakia, had fallen a long way below expectations. They lost the first match 1–3 to England in Bilbao, shining only for a 20-minute spell before the interval. Then, after an easy 4–1 victory over Kuwait in a game best remembered because their opponents threatened to walk off the pitch following a controversial refereeing decision, France struggled to draw 1–1 with Czechoslovakia.

Had it not been for a goalline clearance in the closing minutes of that encounter in Vallodolid, the French team would have been eliminated and returned home instead of travelling to Madrid. But they were not the only side to labour through the early stage and then come good. The same thing happened to World Cup winners Italy.

By the time France went into action in the second stage the line-up had changed considerably from the team beaten by England. There had been a shake-up in defence, mid-field and attack. Injury ruled the star French player, Platini, out of the match with Austria – and perhaps it was his absence which explained why France won by only a single goal, scored by Genghini just before half-time, when they dominated the proceedings and should have had three or four.

We had been eager to get a preview of Platini in the hope of getting some idea of how to cope with him when the time came. A gifted footballer, who was transferred from St Etienne to Italian club Juventus immediately the World Cup ended, Platini is especially noted for his long-range free-kicks.

Like Tottenham's Glenn Hoddle, the Frenchman can strike a free-kick with tremendous power and, at the same time, make the ball swerve in flight. That always presents a problem to an opposing goalkeeper, so I had a special reason for wanting to see Platini perform.

Even without Platini, the Irish 'spies' saw enough to realize the French had a number of talented individuals who would take some stopping. They certainly had more variety than the Yugoslavs and Spaniards we had already faced.

Our prime concern, though, had to be with the Austrians whom we were due to play four days later. They needed to beat us to retain any interest in the World Cup – while we knew that if we lost it would almost certainly be the end of the road for us.

That was the one game I missed. My groin had felt sore during the previous match with Spain and I needed treatment from trainer Jim McGregor in the days which followed. When I told manager Bingham that I still felt uncomfortable, his immediate response was, 'I'll play Jim Platt. There's no sense in taking an unnecessary chance.' Bingham doesn't believe in gambling on a player's fitness if there's any doubt.

So Platt kept goal and George Dunlop took his place on the substitutes' bench, while I was a frustrated onlooker. In many respects I found watching the game with Austria made me more edgy than playing in any of the other matches.

The Austrians were at full strength, but things went well for Northern Ireland in the first half with Billy Hamilton giving us a lead in the 28th minute after that great run by Gerry Armstrong. It looked as if we might be capable of winning by a couple of goals, the result we wanted to give us an advantage over France in the decider.

No sooner had the second half got under way, than the Austrian manager George Schmidt made a couple of substitutions which seemed to rejuvenate his team. Pezzey equalized and one of the subs, Hintermaier, put Austria ahead.

Now it was the Irish team who were really up against it, and with less than 20 minutes left I began to fear our World Cup was virtually over. That's when Hamilton turned up trumps by scoring again, and in a hectic final quarter of an hour it looked as if we might snatch victory. Unfortunately, the lads couldn't quite make it and the game finished 2–2.

It was still an encouraging result in many respects, for we had managed a couple of goals – something no Northern Ireland team had done in any of the previous seven international games in 1982. The fact that Billy Hamilton had scored twice was a terrific boost to his confidence. Billy had grafted so hard and the rest of us were delighted to see him get a deserved reward.

The chance of whether Northern Ireland could reach the World Cup semi-finals for the first time in history now depended on the outcome of the game with France. The odds were stacked against us because we needed to win, but we certainly didn't believe it was an impossible task.

The only team selection doubt was whether I would be OK to play, and two nights before the game Bingham took me aside and said, 'It doesn't look like you will be able to make it.' I didn't share his pessimism, and requested that no decision be made until after a brief training spell on the eve of the match. I got through it with no worries, kicked about 20 balls to prove to myself there was no reaction from the groin and knew I was ready.

Bingham still had to be convinced. He still wasn't sure, and it was trainer McGregor who had the last, and deciding, word: 'Pat will get through the 90 minutes, there's no question about that. If he doesn't, you can blame me – I'll take the responsibility.' It was a smashing gesture by Jim McGregor to go right out on a limb on my behalf, and I really appreciated it. With a vital game only a few hours away it was the kind of vote of confidence which makes any player feel good. So I was picked to play, hopefully to pose extra problems for the French since I had missed the friendly match in Paris earlier in the year.

Alas, our dream of reaching the semi-finals ended that Sunday afternoon in Madrid. The French turned on the style to beat us 4–1. They got the breaks at the right time, and we hardly deserved to lose by such a margin, but they were definitely the better side. Our one complaint was that Martin O'Neill had a smashing goal disallowed, wrongly, for off-side.

Rocheteau, who had originally been dropped against the Austrians and then played most of that match after coming on as a sub, was in the line-up from the start and proved one of the matchwinners. But the truth of the matter is that France had too many stars. We couldn't tie them down and they had that extra yard of pace which made all the difference. We held out until Giresse gave them a lead in the 34th minute – after that we were chasing shadows.

In the second half we had no alternative but to push forward in search of an equalizer. That allowed the French more space and Rocheteau, in particular, revelled in it.

He broke away almost from the half-way line to score the second goal. As he closed in on goal I expected him to take one more step, but he suddenly hit the ball without any backlift. I made a desperate attempt to save, got my fingertips to the ball but couldn't keep it out of the net. On another day, with luck going my way, I might have turned it past the post.

When Rocheteau got through again I thought he was going to try and chip the ball over me, as he had attempted once in the first half. I was stretching my full height when he toe-poked it past me.

Armstrong, who typically never stopped trying even though the cause appeared lost, pulled one back for us to make the score 3–1. But it was too late for a revival and Giresse got another French goal with a header which I felt I did well to reach. I thought I had saved it, but I had pushed the ball against the underside of the bar and it rebounded into the net.

So near and yet so far. It was in stark contrast to the match with Spain, but you can't expect the gods to smile on you all the time. The French were to discover that in their very next outing when they met the Germans in the semi-finals.

The World Cup lasted 22 days for Northern Ireland, from our arrival in Valencia to that defeat by France. So far as I was concerned it was a fabulous experience, and I'm sure the rest of the Irish lads share my feelings.

Maybe it was different for the players of countries like Argentina, Brazil, West Germany and even England, all of whom had set out for Spain in the belief they could win the trophy. Our ambitions had been limited to give a good account of ourselves, and nobody could deny we had brought credit to Ireland.

In future our achievements in the 1982 World Cup will be mentioned in the same breath as the World Cup in Sweden in 1958 when the Northern Ireland team managed by Peter Doherty and captained by Danny Blanchflower exceeded all expectations.

I felt I played well, and derived great personal satisfaction from finally taking part in the tournament after 18 years as an international footballer. I'm told no other player has ever had to wait so long for a World Cup début from the time he made his first appearance for his country.

In fact, I was the third oldest of the 528 players from the 24 nations who travelled to Spain. And how remarkable that the oldest of us all, Italian goalkeeper Dino Zoff, should actually emerge as captain of the winning team. Dino had celebrated his 40th birthday back in February.

Next in line was Belgian mid-field man Wilfried van Moer, who had starred in the 1980 European championships when the Belgians finished as runners-up to West Germany. Wilfried was 37 in March 1982 – three months before me. But van Moer never played in a full game in Spain. He came on as substitute against both El Salvador and Hungary and then, in the second stage, started the match against Poland but was replaced soon after half time.

I was delighted by Zoff's success. Quite apart from the fellow feeling for another veteran, especially another goalkeeper, I do think he made a major contribution to Italy's triumph. He was only called upon to make the occasional good save, but Dino's very presence inspired confidence among his defenders.

Zoff is quite a character, and I had to smile at the fashion in which he totally ignored the four-step rule when he had the ball in his possession. Sometimes it seemed Dino went for a stroll in his own penalty-area, taking up to ten steps without a word of rebuke from any referee. He would have a problem in our First Division now that referees are under instruction to ensure goalkeepers release the ball quickly to avoid any time wasting.

When the World Cup began, few of the critics picked Italy as likely winners, most of the votes going to Brazil, West Germany and Argentina in that order. The Italians had to scuffle through their first group, failing to win a match and drawing in turn with Poland, Peru and the Cameroons. Before the second stage, with Italy bracketed with Argentina and Brazil in Barcelona, I'm told bookmakers were offering prices of up to 40–1 against the Italians collecting the World Cup. But in the end they undoubtedly deserved it.

We all know the Italians can play it either sweet or sour – unfortunately, too often their natural attacking skill is submerged by defensive caution. Maybe their formidable programme in Barcelona caused them to have a go simply because, with the odds stacked so high against them, some of the pressure was off them.

The Italians seemed to adopt an Irish attitude of 'what have we got to lose?' and we saw the best of them in the two victories over Argentina (2–1) and Brazil (3–2). They decided to come out and play, instead of stopping the South Americans playing, and centre-forward Paulo Rossi found his scoring touch when it was most needed.

There was no stopping Italy after that, and they were convincing conquerors of Poland by 2–0 in the semi-final and West Germany 3–1 in the final. I was holidaying in Ireland watching TV when the final took place, and drank a toast to Zoff as he held the World Cup aloft after the presentation. I could only imagine his feeling of fulfilment at that moment. Life may not begin at 40 for a footballer, but it's nice to think it doesn't necessarily end.

Without taking anything from Italy, it's true to say most neutrals had wanted Brazil to succeed in Spain. The reason is simple enough: they are the classic entertainers, and we all like to see football played the Brazilian way. I've never seen another international side who seem to enjoy playing so much.

Those of us who remember the great World Cup winning side of 1970, with Pelé at his peak, looked to the 1982 team to reproduce the same style and go all the way. I thought they would, until the Italians threw a spanner in the works. Then the Brazilians made too many mistakes and were made to pay the price. Perhaps overconfidence was Brazil's ultimate undoing.

Belgium I rated one of the minor successes; an attractive side to watch who provided the opening shock by beating Argentina 1–0. From that point on, the Argentinians never looked as if they would repeat their 1978 performance. They appeared anything but happy and were let down as much by temperament as tactics.

It may not look that way in the record books, but it wasn't a good World Cup for the West Germans either. It seems a crazy statement at first glance, considering they reached the final, but I suspect most German fans would agree with me.

The Germans went to Spain with an impressive pedigree stretching back four years and nobody raised an eyebrow when their manager Jupp Derwall was quoted before the first World Cup-tie with Algeria as saying 'We'll go straight home if we lose this one.' For a nation hardly renowned for a sense of humour, it was a German joke – and it rebounded when Algeria won 2–1.

Derwall's troops didn't retreat back to Germany, of course, but they faced other troubled times. After beating Chile 4–1 in the next game the Germans followed up with a 1–0 win over Austria in Gijon which caused a tremendous uproar. The result enabled both Germany and Austria to reach the second stage, and the Algerians were naturally incensed because they were the principal victims of the score-line.

So the Germans didn't have much goodwill going for them as they progressed to the semi-finals via a 0–0 draw with England and a 2–1 victory over Spain. Then came the meeting with France in Seville and, once again, the Germans ended up with the wrong kind of headlines.

It was a magnificent match, possibly the finest of the entire tournament, which finished 3–3 after extra time before the Germans won a penalty shoot-out to reach the final. Most of the sympathy was with the French, who served up the better football and then unaccountably squandered the 3–1 lead they had built up in the extra half-hour.

But the incident which sparked a storm came after 66 minutes when French full-back Patrick Battiston, who had come on as a substitute just 16 minutes earlier, raced clear towards the German goal and was brought crashing down by a challenge from goalkeeper Harold Schumacher just outside the penalty-area. It was the worst foul of the World Cup, quite blatant since Schumacher seemed to have no chance of getting to the ball. Poor Battiston was carried off on a stretcher, while Schumacher escaped without even a booking when he should have been sent off.

I don't believe any player ever sets out to cripple an opponent, and I think Schumacher was motivated by desperation rather than any evil intent. But he must know in his heart that he should have checked rather than follow through. Schumacher must have regretted that action ever since, and I'm sure I speak for every other goalkeeper when I say I'm glad I wasn't the one involved.

There was an extra 'bonus' for me when we returned from Spain. Together with Sammy Nelson, I was made an honorary member of Warrenpoint Golf Club, not far from Newry. It was an unexpected gesture which I greatly appreciated for, next to football, I rate golf my favourite sport.

16

LOOKING AHEAD

Top-class soccer in England is fast approaching the point when realism will have to take over from sentiment – it is inevitable because of the financial facts of life. The present structure of the Football League, with four divisions and 92 clubs all staffed by full-time professional players, cannot survive much longer.

I hate to say it because I'm essentially a traditionalist. I like the present set-up. I think it is fabulous that clubs such as Brighton, Swansea and Watford have battled through from the bottom to the top and now enjoy First Division football after waiting so long for the chance. But, with the alarming drop in attendances, it is becoming increasingly obvious something drastic has to be done if the game is to last.

Some kind of Super League will have to be formed. Smaller clubs will be forced by economic necessity to introduce part-time players. Reserve football is doomed. Ground sharing and artificial pitches in stadiums with a sliding roof have to be seriously considered in the not-too-distant future. All these innovations will present problems – major problems. But the sombre warning of empty terraces means they have to be tackled, and the sooner the better.

The very idea of a Super League makes a lot of people squirm, and I can understand it. Yet it has got to come, though I don't envy those who have to decide how many clubs it will contain, and just which clubs will be included.

I suspect the lead will have to come from the major clubs themselves; those prepared to form a breakaway league and invite others to join to make up the number. If the big boys do take the initiative, I doubt if you will find many others turning down invitations. The alternative would be to be left in the cold.

Perhaps the first decision which will have to be taken is whether a Super League would be an all-English affair, or extended to include Celtic and Rangers in Scotland.

In England there are seven clubs currently in the First Division who would be automatic members – Arsenal, Aston Villa, Everton, Liverpool, Manchester City, Manchester United and Spurs. They are undoubtedly the aristocrats of soccer, the clubs who would have to act together to point the way. All of them have impressive grounds with the kind of potential support needed to pay top wages.

Picking the clubs to join the 'Magnificent Seven' would be a heart-searching and heat-breaking job. But there would clearly be contenders from the present Second Division such as Chelsea, Newcastle and Sheffield Wednesday.

It would mean considering the claims of Ipswich and Southampton, two clubs which have achieved remarkable success with limited resources but whose crowd-pulling powers are restricted. And what about Queen's Park Rangers, who deserved the highest praise for ambition after transforming a ramshackle ground into a modern stadium?

There are snags in assessing crowd potential. Four years ago, when heralded as the 'Team of the Eighties', Crystal Palace were packing them in each week as they won promotion from the Second Division. In May 1979 more than 50,000 squeezed into Selhurst Park to see Palace make sure of going up by beating Burnley. Three seasons later, back in Division Two, they seldom got 10,000 for any match. Should they be in or out of the Super League?

Barnsley are another example of a lesser light who have shown they can attract big crowds when things are going well at Oakwell. It may sound cruel to exclude the likes of Barnsley and Palace, but one day fairly soon I think it's going to happen.

Once a Super League is formed the first step will be to abolish relegation. There's absolutely no sense in allowing Manchester United to drop out if they finish bottom, when they are the biggest crowd-pullers of all. It would defeat the object of the exercise. Yet, without the threat of going down, would the fans support the sides in the lower half of a Super League in the closing months of a season?

The danger of relegation, in April and May, often pays off at the gate for a threatened club. I recall Spurs getting their two biggest attendances in the last couple of home games in 1974–75, when we were trying to avoid the drop. When we did, by beating Leeds in the final match before a full house at White Hart Lane, I felt as elated as I did after any of my Cup final wins at Wembley.

I appreciate just what it will mean if a Super League comes into existence for those left on the outside looking in. Five years ago I would have thrown up my hands in horror at the idea. Now, sadly, I believe surgery is needed to save the game as Britain's national sport.

When it happens and the remaining clubs re-form, many of them will have to cut costs by renegotiating contracts and employing players on a part-time basis. I only hope it can be done on a gradual basis, starting with the teenagers coming into football, for the majority of older professionals would struggle to find outside jobs in the prevailing economic climate. Few have any qualifications to earn a decent living beyond the game. I'm a typical example.

Most of the present players left school at 16 when they got the opportunity to go into football, and didn't give a thought to A-levels and higher education. So maybe the prospect of part-time soccer would encourage youngsters to continue their studies. It's the advice I would give, anyway, to any lad as an insurance against not making the grade or having his career ended by injury.

I know there are teenagers today with First Division clubs who earn £15,000 or £20,000 a year, but, believe me, they are an élite few, an exception to the rule. I'd prefer to see the majority of youngsters remaining at school until they are 18 before becoming professionals.

The big clubs may have to revamp their youth schemes if players are to come into the game a couple of years later, but I see no reason why the age limit for youth football should not be extended to 20. Often, too much is expected of kids and there are only a few fortunate ones who, like me, become regular League players before reaching their 20th birthday. What is forgotten is the despair of those who are taken on full of hope and then discarded a few years later.

Every League club needs a youth team, now more than ever when clubs are finding it difficult to pay large transfer fees. But do they need a reserve side these days? The answer, in view of the general belt-tightening, has to be 'No, definitely not!' What is more, the public don't want reserve football. So even the 'Super' clubs should cut costs by operating with a first-team squad of 15 or 16 senior players plus a youth set-up.

I am told a First Division club must budget around £100,000 a year for reserve-team expenses, including players' wages, training staff and travel. Yet hardly anybody bothers to turn up to watch reserve football, not even season-ticket holders who, having paid in advance, can occupy their usual seat with no extra charge.

Liverpool seems to me the classic example. They have close on 20,000 season-ticket holders, yet reserve-team crowds on a Saturday at Anfield seldom top 1000 now. It is all the more remarkable because Liverpool have monopolized the Central League, regarded as the best second-team competition of them all, for the past 12 years.

Old-timers will tell you that 10,000 regularly turned up to see Liverpool and Manchester United reserves. West Ham once had 27,000 for
a mid-week Combination fixture with Arsenal just before the war
when the title of that competition was at stake. Arsenal had 22,000 at
Highbury in the early post-war period when England centre-forward
Tommy Lawton played for visitors Chelsea. Even when I started with
Spurs in the mid-sixties and was in and out of the first team, we could
count on crowds of 3000 or so for a home reserve game – more if we
were playing a local 'derby' with Arsenal or West Ham. And you
could be sure that there would always be a few international players
on view.

Those days, before television made an impact with sports pro-
grammes and there was no such thing as *Match of the Day*, have long
since gone. I'm willing to bet that a high proportion of the fans who
watch their first team regularly couldn't even tell you how the reserves
had fared most weeks.

I'm speaking from painful experience after starting season 1982–83
in Arsenal's reserve side. There could hardly have been a greater
contrast to my World Cup duty with Northern Ireland. I soon found
there was no interest and no atmosphere in reserve football. To run
out at Highbury on a Saturday afternoon and see a few hundred people
scattered around the ground is a bit like being hit in the face with a
bucket of cold water.

One of the results of poor reserve attendances is that clubs don't get
value for the wages they are paying players. The usual Arsenal home
attendance for a reserve game wasn't enough to pay my weekly salary,
let alone that of the rest of the team. It certainly affects your performance. You have been training all the week and want to take the game
seriously, but the deserted terraces rob you of any sense of urgency.

If I'm honest, I must admit that I wouldn't want my form assessed
on performances in the second team. I'm sure the majority of senior
players feel the same. I can understand why so many ask for transfers
after being dropped from League football. When you have grown
accustomed to big crowds the feeling is one of anti-climax.

There's no difference between a competitive reserve game and a
practice match at the training ground, and you would be amazed at the
number of talented stars who do not shine in practice matches. They
need the roll of drums which comes with a First Division fixture to
switch on. It's hard to explain, but a big crowd gives you a 15 per
cent lift.

I know I found it more difficult to concentrate keeping goal in a reserve game, with the odd remark from a fan drifting across the ground and heard as clearly as the shouts of the players to each other. In the First Division the buzz of the crowd, sensing danger when opponents build an attack, keeps you constantly alert. It's easier to play in the first team with better players, easier to read a game, for 95 per cent of the time you know what to expect. The opposing centre-forward who mishits a shot in a reserve game can make a monkey out of you.

The majority of reserve-team players today are teenagers, but I can't believe it benefits them to play on empty grounds. With no atmosphere being generated, they are never under the kind of pressure which they have to face when promoted to the first team. They learn nothing more than when playing in youth games. It seems to me that reserve football has outlasted its usefulness to players and clubs.

It would seem much more sensible if clubs got together and shared a stadium when in the same area. I know it goes against tradition, but times are different from when most of the clubs were formed in the last century.

There is no logical reason why it wouldn't work as well as it does in Italy, where Juventus and Torino in Turin, AC Milan and Inter-Milan in Milan and the Rome pair of Lazio and Roma share grounds. They get big crowds, are deadly rivals and training grounds and administrative offices still remain strictly separate.

Some years ago the late Arsenal chairman Denis Hill Wood suggested such a joint venture with Spurs. He was years ahead of his time and the idea came to nothing. But Spurs have since spent a reported five million pounds on building one new grandstand and, without being a student of economics, I find that hard to understand.

The two Sheffield clubs, United and Wednesday, have each spent fortunes on their respective grounds in recent times. Here again, I would have thought that if the cash had been pooled it would have produced a super stadium which could have been used for staging other sporting events and been a boon to the whole community.

The time will come when a perfect artificial surface is manufactured and a new generation of footballers will learn how to play upon it. At the moment there is a natural in-built opposition to such surfaces, even though a number of clubs – including Arsenal – use them for training in indoor arenas. Perhaps that provides a guide to the future, for players are wary of artificial pitches after heavy rain which causes them to slip and slide all over the place. A sliding roof, to be used in the worst winter weather, could make soccer an indoor game in the 21st century.

There could be all sorts of spin-offs from an indoor stadium, for clubs would be able to stage pop concerts, boxing, hockey and basketball matches. Queen's Park Rangers, the only Football League club with an artificial pitch, have already cashed in, in a modest way: for instance, in October 1982 they staged two hockey internationals at Loftus Road on a Saturday morning, prior to playing Shrewsbury Town in a Second Division game. The advantages was that the hockey matches could be planned in advance with no fear of postponement through bad weather, an obvious hazard if another club with a grass pitch had undertaken such a venture.

If there is to be a new modern – indoor? – stadium, I would like to think the Football Association would own it. I have always felt it is scandalous that the FA do not have their own ground. Because of the sad lack of foresight by football's rulers in the past, the FA must have paid for Wembley many times over during the last 60 years.

I've always regarded Wembley as one of the finest stadiums in the world, because there is a touch of magic about the place. But it would have been comforting to think that the vast amount of money taken at the turnstiles had all gone to the FA to be used for the good of the game, instead of a large slice being swallowed up by a private company.

If big-time soccer is played under cover in the future, perhaps it will borrow an idea from another indoor game – a 'Sin Bin' such as that used in Ice Hockey where players can be sent for periods of five or ten minutes after committing an offence. I honestly think that kind of instant punishment would be more acceptable to players than the present system of being booked or sent off and suspended from subsequent games.

I am sure referees would prefer it as well, providing they had the assistance of a time-keeper to check players confined to the 'Sin Bin' in and out. It would eliminate the necessity to write names in a notebook during a game and later send a lengthy report to the FA Disciplinary Committee.

The 'Sin Bin' would be seldom empty these days, as a result of the stricter code of discipline introduced into Football League matches in August 1982, which brought an all-time record number of sendings-off during the 1982–83 season. In my view, and I like to think I can speak from strength because of my good disciplinary record over the past 20 years, it has done football no favours.

Nobody has been able to explain to my satisfaction how the authorities justified taking a tougher line when the Laws of the Game have remained unaltered. By deciding to interpret them in a different way, it strikes me that referees have been asked to get round the rules rather than enforce them.

Sending off a player for handling the ball (including a goalkeeper if he does so outside the penalty-area) seems absolutely crazy, especially when this hitherto undiscovered 'law' only operates in Britain and not in the rest of the soccer world. The inconsistency has frustrated players, for it seems that the punishment meted out depends upon which particular referee is in charge. And why should a goalkeeper be ordered off if he brings down an opposing forward outside the area, yet probably escape if the same incident happens inside the 'box' and a penalty awarded? Since the forward has a better chance of scoring once inside the area, and nearer to goal, it doesn't make sense.

Another example of the Laws of the Game being interpreted in a different way concerns the old-fashioned shoulder charge. It was once part and parcel of soccer, and in my early days I was often hit fairly and squarely by forwards when I caught the ball. Now referees simply don't allow it. As a goalkeeper I ought to be thankful, but I always felt I could take care of myself. Anyway, forwards have become more cunning now, and try to obstruct a goalkeeper in possession instead of actually making contact. It is one more example of gamesmanship, requiring a sharp-eyed referee to spot it in a crowded goalmouth.

One reason why the increase in the number of players sent off – and I do not excuse those who make a vicious tackle or swap punches – disturbs me is that I feel it reduces soccer as a spectacle and robs the spectators of enjoyment. I can't believe fans want to see one team with 11 and another with 10, nine or even eight men. It ruins a game and there is less satisfaction in beating a depleted side. Even if you've won, you know deep down you haven't really won on merit.

I wonder if the clamp-down on tackling will boomerang on British teams in both international matches and European club games. Football is an instinctive business: you can't play one way one week and another way the next week.

Hustling, getting sharp tackles in and bundling the ball away has always been a basic ingredient of the British game and our methods have generally proved successful. It's a fact of life that 80 per cent of continental players are superior technically, but they have always respected the British for their spirit, strength and stamina. Most of all, they respect us for our power in the tackle.

Even the top continental clubs do not relish being drawn against English teams in European competitions, and the success of Liverpool, Nottingham Forest and Aston Villa in the premier tournament, the European Cup, has reinforced the merits of our traditional style. Now I fear something is being taken from the British game, for I don't think that a team allowed to make 20 or 30 passes without a tackle – while, presumably, opponents wait for them to make a mistake – is what British fans want to see. It just isn't football as we know it.

It is sad to admit that players may have helped to bring the new disciplinary system on themselves by the 'acting' which has gone on in recent years, with a player rolling over as though he had both legs broken after a mild challenge – then regaining his feet and chasing around immediately after being awarded a free-kick. That has always made me cringe, and I feel ashamed when such an incident is shown on television. Any Rugby player watching must think we are a bunch of poufs.

I've never understood the mentality of the player who wants to get an opponent into trouble with the referee. I was brought up in Gaelic football always to turn the other cheek. If you were hurt the last thing you wanted was to let the other fellow see it. Even if every bone in your body was aching, you tried to keep going to prove you could take it. That's the kind of honest attitude I'd like every professional footballer to adopt. Then maybe a referee's job in spotting the serious fouls would be made easier.

I have said a lot about the future of soccer, but what about the future of Pat Jennings? Time is running out for me as a player, so it is clearly something I have to think about. Hopefully, I can last for another couple of seasons. I know I'm still good enough and fit enough to do that, but I won't need anybody to tell me when the moment comes to hang up my gloves. I've no intention to try and live on my reputation in a lower division if I can't give value for money.

I would like to stay involved in football and make use of the experience I've gained during the last 20 years. I don't see myself as a manager, although given the chance to serve as an assistant I would be tempted to see if I was cut out for the job. But obviously my chief asset is my goalkeeping skills and know-how, and I would like the opportunity to pass some of that on to up-and-coming youngsters.

I feel I've got a lot to offer. I've had more international games than any British goalkeeper and more experience of European football at club level than 95 per cent of keepers. I'm not renowned as a great talker, but I have no doubt I could put my ideas over to others – whether they be professional players or schoolchildren.

So far as I'm aware, there is no special coaching diploma for goal-keepers. Yet it is a specialized business. Outfield players haven't got a clue on how to instruct goalkeepers, and even those loaded with coaching badges will admit it if they're honest.

When I arrived at Watford from Newry as a 17-year-old, there was nobody around to tell me how to do my job. Bill McGarry, when he became manager, was brutally frank about it. 'I can't tell you what to do,' he said; 'I've never been a goalkeeper, it's all double Dutch to me.' I could have done with some advice at that time, yet I admired Bill for levelling with me instead of perhaps misleading me with the wrong kind of advice.

In those days I sometimes got the impression that goalkeepers were just there to make the numbers up, but now I feel they are treated with greater respect. Even the way transfer fees for keepers soared, to beyond £500,000 when West Ham signed Phil Parkes, is an indication of our improved status.

I have learned something from the special goalkeeping sessions at Arsenal twice a week under Bob Wilson, in itself a new trend in pro-fessional football. Manchester United employed former Northern Ireland international Harry Gregg as a goalkeeper coach for a spell and now England manager Bobby Robson is making use of the knowledge of Alan Hodgkinson, the old England and Sheffield United keeper.

It is important that any coaching is undertaken by somebody who has proved himself in the past and is still able to demonstrate what he wants his students to do. Anybody who goes for golf lessons, and then finds the instructor can't hit the ball cleanly, soon loses interest. Blackboard theory has its uses, but it has to be backed up by the ability to go out on a pitch and follow any talk with action.

So, when my playing career is over, I like to think there will be League clubs who feel that Pat Jennings can help to develop their goalkeepers; and that I can pass something on to those kids, still at school, who want to follow in my footsteps. The idea of coaching a group of, say, 12-year-olds excites me. It must be a wonderful feeling to spot a lad who looks like he has the potential to make the First Division grade. Equally, there must be a great deal of satisfaction in seeing an improvement in a youngster who starts out all fingers and thumbs.

Many children dream of sporting glory. I know I did when I used to go to Windsor Park, Belfast, to watch Northern Ireland play. I remember vividly one afternoon climbing on the lower rung of a floodlight pylon in torrential rain and watching a game against Scotland. I left the ground soaked to the skin, but I was too busy with my thoughts of one day being good enough to represent my country to bother about a minor detail like possible pneumonia.

I've been one of the lucky ones – that's why I would like to put something back into the game. I don't want to be one of those old professionals I occasionally meet who tell me they never go to watch football. I find that rather sad.

Soccer, to me, is still the greatest game of all. I only wish I was starting out all over again.

FIRST-CLASS CAREER AT A GLANCE 1962-63 TO 1982-83

SEASON	CLUB	TABLE	HONOURS	Lg	LgC	FA	UEFA	ECWC	NI	TOTAL
1962-63	Watford	17		2	—	—	—	—	—	2
1963-64	Watford	3		46	1	3	—	—	2	52
1964-65	Spurs	6		23	—	—	—	—	6	29
1965-66	Spurs	8		22	—	3	—	—	5	30
1966-67	Spurs	3	FA Cup	41	1	8	—	—	2	52
1967-68	Spurs	7		42	—	5	—	4	3	54
1968-69	Spurs	6		42	6	4	—	—	6	58
1969-70	Spurs	11		41	1	4	—	—	4	50
1970-71	Spurs	3	League Cup	40	6	5	—	—	5	56
1971-72	Spurs	6	UEFA Cup	41	7	5	12	—	5	70
1972-73	Spurs	8	League Cup	40	10	3	10	—	6	69
1973-74	Spurs	11	UEFA Cup (r/u)	36	—	1	10	—	4	51
1974-75	Spurs	19		41	1	2	—	—	6	50
1975-76	Spurs	9		40	6	2	—	—	7	55
1976-77	Spurs	22		23	1	1	—	—	7	32
1977-78	Arsenal	5	FA Cup (r/u)	42	7	6	—	—	3	58
1978-79	Arsenal	7	FA Cup	39	1	11	6	—	9	66
1979-80	Arsenal	4	FA Cup (r/u); ECWC (r/u)	37	7	11	—	9	3	67
1980-81	Arsenal	3		31	2	1	—	—	4	38
1981-82	Arsenal	5		16	4	1	4	—	8	33
1982-83	Arsenal	—		4	1	—	—	—	—	5
				689	62	76	42	13	95	977*

*This figure does not include Great Britain against Europe; 2 Charity Shield appearances; 2 Texaco Cup ties; and 2 Anglo Italian Cup Winners' Cup ties which raise the total to 984 first-class matches played up to 31 December 1982.